PUMPING UP!

Super Shaping the Feminine Physique

PUMPING UP!

Super Shaping the Feminine Physique

Ben Weider, C.M., & Robert Kennedy

 Sterling Publishing Co., Inc.   New York

EDITED BY ROBERT HERNANDEZ
DESIGNED BY JIM ANDERSON

Library of Congress Cataloging in Publication Data

Weider, Ben, 1923–
 Pumping up!

 Includes index.
 1. Bodybuilding for women.   I. Kennedy, Robert,
1938–   II. Title.
GV546.6.W64W43   1985   646.7′5   84-26852
ISBN 0-8069-4190-1
ISBN 0-8069-7984-4 (pbk.)

Copyright © 1985 by Ben Weider and Robert Kennedy
Published by Sterling Publishing Co., Inc.
387 Park Avenue South, New York, N.Y. 10016
Distributed in Canada by Sterling Publishing
℅ Canadian Manda Group, P.O. Box 920, Station U
Toronto, Ontario, Canada M8Z 5P9
Distributed in Great Britain and Europe by Cassell PLC
Artillery House, Artillery Row, London SW1P 1RT, England
Distributed in Australia by Capricorn Ltd.
P.O. Box 665, Lane Cove, NSW 2066

Contents

In 1934 a penniless twelve-year-old kid lifted
his first barbell and immediately felt the better for
it. Within a year he was stronger, fitter, bigger,
and then a wildly ambitious thought suddenly
came to his mind: "What if I started a
magazine, and devoted my life to promoting
bodybuilding as a sport and a way of life?"
It is to that single thought that the
authors wholeheartedly dedicate this book.
The kid's name was Joseph Weider.

Acknowledgments

The enormous popularity of women's bodybuilding is more evident today than ever before in the history of womankind.

This phenomenon is due mainly to the insight and promotion of one individual—Joe Weider. He saw the potential for a new sport, studied the requirements, and made a positive series of decisions to put women's bodybuilding on the map. Muscle & Fitness, *his hugely successful publication, spread the word, making bodybuilding for women a worldwide activity, known by everyone, practiced by millions, and idolized by the media.*

It is Joe Weider to whom we all owe a debt of sincere appreciation. We would also like to thank him for allowing us to use pictures from his photo library.

We acknowledge the following photographers for their excellent work: Michael Neveux, Peter Brenner, Luc Ekstein, Bob Gardner, Reg Bradford, Bruce Curtis, Bill Dobbins, Dick Zimmerman, Harry Langdon, Steve Douglas, Doris Barrilleaux, and Bill Heimanson.

Special thanks to our editor at Sterling, Robert Hernandez, and to Jim Anderson, the designer of the book.

The beautiful Rachel McLish and bodybuilding entrepreneur Joe Weider

Introduction

Believe it! You can use weights and barbells to sculpt your body in the same way that a sculptor uses his or her hammer and chisel to create a work of art.

Simply visualize the way you want to be and get to work. Add a little here—take off a bit there. Lose weight, gain weight. Shape up, slim down, add muscle, and lose fat. Whatever it takes, the bodybuilding way of life has the answer, and it will do the job faster than any other method known to women everywhere.

The beauty of weights is that you can *tailor* the resistance to your condition. In other words, if you are excessively thin and weak, you can start by using extremely light weights so that you slowly ease yourself into condition. As you tone up, lose fat, and improve your shape, you will be able to add a little more weight to the bar. Gradually, with a little patience, you will accomplish your dream. You will obtain your optimal condition and physical appearance.

Ms. Olympia 1984 Cory Everson

Candy Csencsits

This publication on bodybuilding for women exists because the authors, with a combined 80 years of experience in the field, sincerely believe that weight training, according to the principles in this book, is the most effective way known to shape up the female body.

The Beauty of Flex Appeal

The lovely Rachel McLish has done a tremendous amount of good for the women's bodybuilding movement. It was her body that inspired the coined phrase *flex appeal*. Indeed, Rachel went on to write a very successful book of that same name.

Do you have any reservations about the current women's bodybuilding look? Many still do. It could be argued that more women would still rather look like Victoria Principal than Rachel McLish or Gladys Portugues. Even Betty Weider freely admitted in an article in *Muscle & Fitness* that she sees women with muscular bodies that she doesn't particularly like.

Remember, *you* are in charge of the weights. *You* are using them as tools to sculpt your body to physical perfection. Use them according to our recommendations and the benefits will amaze you.

Progressive-resistance exercise apparatus and, more particularly, weights are sometimes referred to as *iron pills*. Today's doctors, scientists, coaches, and physical educators are in agreement about the enormous capabilities and advantages that can be gained from the regular use of barbells and dumbbells. If indeed weights *were* pills, they would be known as magic pills. The benefits gained through their regular use are little short of miraculous.

We will say it *once* more here (we would like to write it across the sky in mile-high letters).

I have heard the question many times. "You wouldn't want to look like that would you?" And it has always seemed to me that what the questioner really meant was: "Don't you agree that women who display that kind of muscularity look awful?"

Taking the question at face value, I can truthfully say, "I would not want to look like that." The bodybuilding physique, whether it be men or women, is very specialized. You can admire it without wanting to emulate it, just as you can be a big fan of gymnastics without wanting to train as a gymnast.

When you first see a picture of a woman bodybuilder or if you attend a contest, you could find the experience strange. If you are not used to seeing muscles on women, with the attendant low body-fat appearance, then you may not be totally committed to the cause. You could even think it looks unnatural.

Actually, when you get used to seeing really great female physiques you will come to realize the true beauty of a completely trained feminine body. To our mind there is no sport—be it rowing, swimming, tennis, skating, running, or gymnastics—that builds and shapes a woman's body so perfectly as weight training.

When fashion experts compare their top models with the likes of Candy Csencsits, Lydia Cheng, Carla Dunlap, Rachel McLish, and Gladys Portugues, they are forced to concede that it's "no contest" when it comes to physical beauty. The trained bodybuilder wins hands down. Not even a *variety* of sports, even when coupled with the natural vitality and advantage of youth can duplicate the overall aesthetics of a correctly weight-trained body.

We cannot characterize women's bodybuilding in one sentence. There are too many factors. Individuals differ greatly in their skeletal proportions and aptitude for adding muscle. Some women will have wide or slim hips, narrow or wide shoulders, long or short legs. The point is that scientific bodybuilding, as explained in this book, can help you harden up, balance up, and look dynamic.

There is no such thing as the perfect physique. But if you are serious about sculpting your body, your dedication will get you as near to perfection as humanly possible.

If you are not yet convinced of the beauty of women's bodybuilding, look again. Study the pictures in this book. Above all . . . remember this: You don't have to be big. You are in control here. Develop your body to the degree that you wish. As in fashion, styles in bodybuilding are always changing. Dumbbells and barbells are your tools. You can create your own style. The beauty of flex appeal is in the eyes of the beholder.

Cory Everson, Dinah Anderson, Rachel McLish, and Mary Roberts await the judges' decision at the 1984 Ms. Olympia contest in Montreal, Canada.

Abbye "Pudgy" Stockton, one of the first hardcore female bodybuilders who gained prominence in the '50s, poses with Steve Reeves.

WOMEN'S BODYBUILDING

Georgia Miller-Fudge

A Brief History

David Webster of Scotland, a well-known historian on the topic of weight training, has established that weights were used by women to shape and improve their physical appearance, health, and strength as long ago as 3600–3500 B.C., when the great Emperor Yu-Kang Chi made his subjects exercise every day with dumbbells.

Lisa Lyon has always been an advocate for women's bodybuilding.

In ancient Egypt, one of the oldest empires, illustrated walls of the Beni Hassan dated from 3400 B.C. clearly show bodybuilding exercises being done with weights, which were usually made from marble or lead. All this happened well over 5,000 years ago.

In more recent times, women's bodybuilding was only practiced by a very small percentage of individuals, and these women used weights only because they had become "believers" as a result of being married to a bodybuilder or having a brother or other relation who was into the sport. Very few women indeed had the confidence to train with weights unless they were related in some way to a male bodybuilder. Those few who did it on their own were regarded as weird.

At the turn of the century, following in the popularity of Eugen Sandow, numerous women used weights in stage performances, showing off their lifting prowess as well as their impressive muscles. Audiences thrilled at the lifting feats of notable strong women such as Katie Sandowina, Athleta, and Minerva, among others.

When the darling of vaudeville Eugen Sandow died prematurely in October 1925 (of peritonitis at the age of 58) the strong-man/strong-woman era faded into obscurity. Films captured a great deal of the live stage audience and the harsh realities of World War II overshadowed the frivolities of such things as exercising for physical improvement. If people trained for anything, it was for survival from the horrors of warfare, not the enhancement of the body beautiful.

When peace was declared bodybuilding saw a mild recovery. Along with the influx of men (mainly in California) taking up bodybuilding, a small number of women started weight training, too. Abbye "Pudgy" Stockton was one of the better-known iron slingers. She was proud of her strength and never hesitated to flex her muscles for the Santa Monica muscle-beach crowd.

Abbye appeared in bodybuilding periodicals and even had her own column in

Shelley Gruwell poses at an early physique contest before increased muscular development was the style for women.

Strength and Health magazine. According to International Federation of Bodybuilding (IFBB) historian Steve Wennerstrom, "Abbye Stockton helped set the stage for women of the future in their quest for muscular fitness."

Abbye was joined by an ever-increasing number of enthusiasts who openly recognized the usefulness of progressive-resistance exercise—Relno Brewer McCrea, Grena Trumbo, Peggy Gironda, Edna Rivers, Vera Christenson, and many others. Virtually every woman had come by her training as a result of being married to a successful bodybuilder.

As men's bodybuilding gained momentum in the '50's, '60s, and '70s, their contests were often supplemented by the inclusion of a women's "beauty contest." The general consensus was that the females added a pleasant relief to the serious task of viewing and judging the men. Clearly these competitions had little to do with women's bodybuilding as we know it today. In fact, they were often viewed by the boisterous audience, giving rise to catcalls and ear-piercing whistles.

Then something happened. Because the female entrants were invariably subjected to what amounted to chauvinistic and sexist abuse, very few women could be coaxed into entering. In order to keep the contests going, promoters would often solicit almost any female, and for a while it seemed as though the majority of contestants were being enrolled from the sleazier side of show business.

It wasn't long, however, before the competing male bodybuilders started to enter their wives and girlfriends in answer to the promoter's call for women entrants, and it didn't take the judges too long to realize that the women who weight-trained actually had superior physiques. This was particularly evident in Britain where the annual Mr. Universe show held a women's contest in conjunction with the men's event. Ninety-five percent of the women who entered this contest, inappropriately named "Miss Bikini," were weight-trained, and they looked it. When you compared their physiques to those seen in traditional beauty pageants, there was simply no contest.

While Jacqueline Nubret, Christine Zane, and Cindy Shakespear were winning contests in Europe, Sandy Nista and April Nicotra were doing the same in North America. The common denominator of each was that they had trained extensively with weights. These were the early days of women's bodybuilding. April Nicotra in 1976 became Miss USA and Cindy Shakespear won the Miss World title.

Just one year later bodybuilding's first women's competition would take place, marking the end of the beauty shows in association with men's events. Now the women had gained equality.

Writing in *Flex* magazine, Steve Wennerstrom talked of the event: "It took place without much ballyhoo, in Canton, Ohio, in November 1977. The winner of the contest was Gina LaSpina, and there is no doubt that this was a women's bodybuilding contest."

The promoter/creator of that show was an energetic fellow named Henry McGhee; as an employee of the Canton YMCA, he informed competitors that they would be judged "like the men" with emphasis on muscular development, symmetry, and physique presentation. In addition, McGhee founded an organization known as the United States Women's Physique Association (USWPA) to help organize women interested in bodybuilding competition. He published the newsletter *Sartorius*, which upheld his purpose, "to overcome the limited, beauty queen stereotype of what the American woman should look like."

Both McGhee's newsletter and his organization ceased to exist by 1980, but his original contribution to women's bodybuilding competition is firmly entrenched in the annals of the sport.

In 1979, Doris Barrilleaux founded an organization called the Southeastern Physique Association (SPA) with its own newsletter, *Spa News*. (Later her organization became the Superior Physique Association, still retaining the same initials.)

At this time, Florida was the hotbed of women's bodybuilding, the training ground of such physiques as those of Kathy Lewis, Suzanne Kosak, Pam Brooks, Laura Combes,

Susan Bressler, Georgia Miller-Fudge, and Doris Barrilleaux herself. These bodybuilders, all ardent iron pumpers, would enter shows whenever possible.

One of the SPA recommendations was that their women compete without shoes or other accoutrements . . . yet in shows, such as Dan Lurie's Miss Body Beautiful, NABBA's Miss Bikini, and George Snyder's Best in the World (1979), high-heeled shoes were required during the onstage presentation. Travelling from Florida to New York in 1979, SPA member Georgia Miller-Fudge created a bit of a stir when she defiantly took off her shoes prior to performing her free-posing routine at Dan Lurie's Miss Body Beautiful contest. As she stepped up onto the rostrum she was greeted with wild applause.

Women's bodybuilding had arrived. The media covered the subject with enthusiasm. Doris Barrilleaux and her gang appeared on the television show "Real People." Merv Griffin interviewed Lisa Lyon and Stacy Bentley, and even *Time* magazine featured an article on women's bodybuilding.

To keep up with the incredible surge in growth of women's bodybuilding, new magazines on the subject were created, the Ms. Olympia title was established (the highest professional honor and usually the most lucrative), and the IFBB created a women's committee at its 1979 congress in Columbus, Ohio. Christine Zane was elected the first chairperson to serve as the head of the newly formed committee, the purpose of which was to facilitate further organization.

At the beginning of the 1980s bodybuilding for women had an official home, with outlets to the rest of the world. Couple this with the women's coverage in Joe Weider's *Muscle & Fitness* magazine and the indomitable tenacity of the female trainers and success was assured. Almost overnight women's bodybuilding swept the globe, and *Life* magazine described it in a cover story as the *world's fastest-growing sport of the '80s.*

Women's bodybuilding is here to stay.

SIZING UP YOUR BODY

Rachel McLish stretches out prior to training.

Honest Self-Evaluation

Self-evaluation is an important part of bodybuilding because it gives you a base from which to work. Yes, even the sculptor has to start with something (usually a shapeless hunk of wood or stone). You must begin with the shape that your body is in right now.

How fit are you? How fat are you? Are you underweight? Are you healthy? Ask yourself these questions.

Very few people are truly in touch with their physical condition or their physical appearance. If you ask a fit person what type of

Diana Dennis

condition she is in, you may well get the answer, "Terrible, I need more exercise." On the other hand, you could ask a totally unfit person the same question and get a resounding, "I'm as fit as a fiddle!"

If you are in doubt about your present appearance, try the mirror test. Take all your clothes off and stand in front of a full-length mirror. Turn all the lights on. Do this at a time when you are completely alone. You don't want any distractions. Cast your eyes across your shoulders; look at your arms, chest, waistline; take in your hips, upper legs, and calves. Check your overall proportions. Are your lower legs big enough? Have you too much weight on the upper thigh area? Is there fat around your lower back? Are your upper arms a lot thicker near the shoulders than they are near the elbows? Now try to decide what you want to correct. Is your posture good? Are you too fat?

The surest way of finding out if you have too much fat under your skin is to try the pinch test (medically known as the skinfold test).

Simply pinch some of your skin between your thumb and forefinger. The best sites are the triceps (back of the upper arm), side of waist, top of thigh, or side of chest. If your pinched skin is more than half an inch, this is an indication that you are carrying too much fat.

Remember, fat destroys shape. It fills in the areas where one muscle curves into another. Fat spoils the natural curve running from the waist to the hips. It ruins the descending silhouette from the hips to the knees. There should not be a mound of fat on the upper outer thigh. The knees, together with the ankles and wrists, should always be bony and virtually devoid of fat. This boniness in the legs particularly emphasizes the curves of the thigh and calf muscles. Superfluous fat in the knee and ankle area will give your leg a straight, uninteresting appearance.

One way of discovering how you look is to have someone take a few Polaroid pictures of

Debbie Duncanson stretches out her back and hamstring muscles.

you. Within a minute or two you will be able to sit down and closely scrutinize your physical condition. You can even compare yourself with pictures of women noted for their great bodies in magazines or with pictures of yourself when you were younger. The important thing is that you become totally *aware* of how good or bad you look. *Learn* about yourself. Try to determine what your ideal weight should be. Find out exactly how much fat you have on your legs, hips, waist, and shoulders. Keep aware of your physical appearance and half the battle is won.

It may be harder to evaluate your physical fitness. Obviously, if you can run up a few flights of stairs without being unduly out of breath, then you are probably fit. On the other hand, if you feel bad after walking a block or two, then you are in trouble.

Whatever your own personal feelings are towards your current fitness level, it is strongly recommended that you ask your doctor to give you a physical stress test. Tell him (or her) the type of exercise you'll be doing. Show your doctor this book by all means. It is always advisable before undertaking any type of exercise or nutrition program to have a *complete medical checkup*. You will find that a stress test can be fun (you will probably have to step up and down on some boxes or jog on a machine while your breathing and pulse rate are monitored). After you get the "go ahead" from your doctor, you'll be thrilled that you have a clean bill of health.

Alternatively, should an irregularity be uncovered, you're still ahead, because you can take steps to correct any malfunction discovered by the testing.

Whatever you do, resist the temptation to suddenly throw yourself into a furious session of formal exercise. Remember, we are going to coax, not pound your body into a new dy-

Gladys Portugues

namic shape. We do not want you to be hampered by exercise aches and pains because you neglected to take the advice given here. Your new body will assuredly develop—but do the job right and follow the steps: start at the beginning.

One of the advantages of bodybuilding is that nearly *everyone*—not just the sublimely coordinated—can do it. However, it can pose a problem to those with heart or circulatory disorders such as high-blood pressure or other organic malfunctions. So be sure to check with your doctor if in doubt.

The Age Factor

Men usually discover bodybuilding between the ages of sixteen to nineteen. The reason is simple. They are tired of being skinny and laughed at. Women, on the other hand, often start to exercise only when they see a deterioration in their condition. This usually begins when they first notice those dreaded signs of adipose tissue—fat!

Thousands of men also take up bodybuilding to lose flab, and untold numbers of skinny women want to add flesh to their limbs. However, most ladies undertake a program of formal exercise for one reason: to lose excess weight and to tone up their bodies.

Many of these women will be asking the questions: Is it too late? Am I too old? We have been asked these questions not just by people in their forties and seventies, but by people in their twenties and thirties. And even in their teens!

There is *no* exact age at which to start bodybuilding. You can be a teenager, middle aged, or elderly. All you have to do is follow the advice of this book carefully and tailor the exercises to your present condition and needs. The urge to get into shape can hit you at any stage in life, and age does not automatically disqualify you.

One of the nice things about bodybuilding is that it erases your fear of the bathroom scale. Women have dieted for ages, basing

Shelley Gruwell

their evaluation of their physiques on scales, instruments designed to measure pounds only, not the difference between the body's muscle and fat content. If you are not already aware of it, muscle weighs more than fat. This means that you can actually weigh more while losing fat because you are adding muscle as the fat is discarded.

Women who work out seldom worry about what the scales say. It is the mirror that counts. A body is judged by its shape, not by its weight!

Once you have carefully evaluated your present condition, then develop what Lisa Lyon calls "clear vision." Set your goals realistically and map out your journey to success. Clear vision means: Translating your needs and desires into reality *without* wasting energy on anxiety, *without* constantly asking, "Am I doing the right thing?" Don't allow negative influences to destroy your dreams of physical perfection and superstardom.

Facts and Fiction

Whereas a woman's progress in bodybuilding does not equal, or very seldom equals, that of a man, it should also be recognized that women do not have to *achieve* as much as men. The average man may weigh 150 pounds with 12-inch arms and a 38-inch chest. To become a champion bodybuilder he will have to increase those statistics to approximately a 200-pound bodyweight, 19-inch arms, and a 50-inch chest.

In modern competition, at the highest level, little benefit is gained by a woman who has arms bigger than 14–15 inches, and certainly chest size and bodyweight have little bearing on the degree of excellence she may be accorded.

If size is not the aim in women's physical culture, then what is? Surely the term *bodybuilding* means building the body. Both men and women build their bodies in this sport, but that is no reason to assume that building up size is the only aspect of the sport. It is just *one* of the elements. Of equal importance are the achievement of a proportionate build, the elimination of superfluous fat, and the overall toning of every muscle of the physique.

Far from wanting to *build* their bodies, many newcomers to weight training (progressive-resistance exercise) actually want to take off weight rather than build it up.

So what can you expect from regular exercise with barbells and dumbbells?

According to Joyce Vedral, Ph.D., "By following the bodybuilding lifestyle, you can quickly and efficiently improve your appearance, health, physical fitness, mental outlook, and your sex appeal."

Working with weights increases endurance and flexibility and improves your

Rachel McLish demonstrates how the incline bench press develops the pectoral muscles of the chest.

heart and lung functions. Dr. Nagler, Physiatrist-in-Chief at the Cornell Medical Center in New York City, offers another plus: "As women get older, they tend to stoop at the shoulders. Bodybuilding helps them maintain an erect posture for a much longer time by keeping the back extensor muscles strong."

A recent study published in *The Physician and Sports Medicine* magazine indicated that women athletes who trained with weights were three times less likely to be injured in sports-related activities. It was also noted that if injuries *did* occur, the weight-training group recuperated twice as quickly as those who did not. The reasons? Improved muscle control guards against injury; greater overall strength gives more support to the other parts of the body and helps you withstand abuse. The study also reported that competitive women bodybuilders are "somewhat *less* anxious, neurotic, depressed, angry, confused, and *more* vigorous, extroverted, and self-motivated than the general population."

Naturally, you will come up against the muscle myths—the most common one being that weight training will turn you into a musclebound freak. This is just not true. When it comes to building man-sized biceps, most women don't have enough of what it takes—namely, man-sized levels of testosterone, the male hormone responsible for muscle growth. So unless you have above-average amounts of this hormone, and only if you are prone to general hulkiness, you'll never be mistaken for Lou Ferrigno's bodyguard. Progressive exercise will lead to improved muscle tone, and with high-intensity workouts you will be able to increase muscle size to a degree. In most areas you will only add limited size.

There's nothing to be afraid of when you take up bodybuilding. There are no undesirable side effects from weight training. It is a healthy pursuit, one that complements other pastimes. Vigorous exercise helps your mind to function at its best and conditions you for other games and sports.

Rachel McLish sports the coveted Joe Weider Medallion.

The bodybuilding way of living is so exciting because the well-being and appearance-enhancing factors are undeniable. Let us simply bid you to read on. This book will unfold the wonders of pumping iron. We show you exactly how to completely remould your body to a new dynamic shape. Your dreams are ready to be fulfilled.

GETTING STARTED

Bodybuilder Gladys Portugues of New York City

Controlled Ambition

Most likely, there's something inside you that yearns to possess a strong, shapely body. Right now, you would like to be *into* working out but you don't know how to start. Every day we see an influx of hundreds, perhaps thousands of new women to the sport. If you are a beginner to bodybuilding, there is one thing we know for sure: You are confused!

Bodybuilding is not an exact science. Not only will you read of different rules in bodybuilding, but you may well see them in the same magazine. As is often the case, the most rigid opinions are held by those with the least knowledge. True, rules are made to be broken, but there are basic dos and don'ts which will give you the best chance of success.

Beginners seek the fastest, surest, and safest way to build muscle size, strength, vigorous health, and well-being. Often going at it choose the wrong path at the beginning of your journey, you may never get to your destination.

Bodybuilding for the beginner must be simple. It should involve workouts that are relatively short so that sufficient recuperative time is allowed for the broken-down muscle cells to repair themselves. You must eat well regularly and get adequate sleep.

So there you have it: exercise, food, and rest. Get them right and you are on your way.

Rachel McLish and Carla Dunlap are both former Ms. Olympias.

on their own or taking bad advice, they achieve virtually the opposite effect. Their training progress is slowed or nonexistent, and they end up tired and disenchanted with the whole scene, often giving up in disgust at not being able to succeed. Remember, the shortest route is the correct route. If you

The principles we are laying down here are not the last word: There is always room for various ideas and differing opinions. We suggest, however, that you stick to our advice in the beginning, and don't allow yourself to be influenced by what others say or by whatever else you may read. Stay on track with us

Ms. Olympia Cory Everson performs a single-arm dumbbell exercise.

now and your initiation into the iron game will be relatively problem free.

Your first workout is important in more ways than one. Training with weights is the most concentrated form of exercise known. Your first few workouts should be performed with very light weights. Unless you are natu-

rally strong and well-conditioned right this minute, use *only* the bar for your first workout. In time, as you gain strength, you will add some discs for added resistance in almost all your exercises.

Sets and Reps

Sets and reps (repetitions) are two words which you need to know, because they are the fundamental terminology of weight training.

When you perform an exercise, say for ten counts and then replace the weights on the floor for a breather, that is known as one *set*. These counts or repetitions are known as *reps*. If you do three sets of twelve reps, it is usually written as 3×12. Two sets of fifteen repetitions will appear as 2×15.

Beginners should only do *one* set of each exercise. After a short period (10–14 days) you can graduate to two sets per exercise and very soon after that (another week or two) you may find yourself wanting to do three or even four sets per exercise.

Naturally, beginners should not push their bodies to the maximum by rushing from one set of exercise to another. The normal criteria is to perform your next set when your breathing has returned to normal and your body has settled down somewhat from the previous series of repetitions. You will find that in heavy exercises, such as squats, you will require a longer rest period (a few minutes) than you would between less strenuous exercises (60–90 seconds). In many cases, as a contest approaches it is usual practice to progressively lessen the amount of rest you take between sets. This serves to place more stress on the muscles over a shorter period of time, and is another form of creating additional intensity. There is also a slight aerobic effect from increasing workout pace, another way of burning more calories and reducing body fat.

Candy Csencsits takes advantage of some aerobic exercise.

Correct Breathing

Deliberate, forceful breathing during exercise is important and serves several functions. It supplies the system with essential oxygen at the needed rate, preventing an oxygen "debt." Without deep breathing you could run out of air, get dizzy, and lose concentration. You could even faint.

Regular breathing also enables you to use more weight in your exercises and helps to focus your attention on the performance of the movements. It gives your exercises cadence and rhythm, which are other important aspects of successful bodybuilding. There is general agreement that in most exercises you should inhale quickly during the easiest part of an exercise and exhale just as the hardest part is accomplished.

Because weight-training movements are usually done briskly, once you have gotten used to the exercises, you should inhale and exhale through your mouth. Gulp in your air. Then blow it out between pursed lips. Some bodybuilders even make a practice of noisily whistling as they exhale. This reminds them to keep their rhythm, and the cadence is more obvious. It may, however, be distracting to others in a gym, but it does help keep your exercise rhythm under control.

Aerobic Exercise

This specific form of exercise depends on the body's use of oxygen. Weight training is used to sculpt your muscles. Aerobic exercise is used to condition your organs and circulatory system—the lungs and heart particularly. Every health-minded woman should practice some form of aerobic exercise. There have been millions of words written on the subject, but aerobic exercise is very simple. It is the repetition of an ongoing movement, such as swimming, rowing, hill climbing, walking, cycling, cross-country skiing, skating, or jogging for a period of 20–30 minutes, whereby your heart rate is elevated but does not exceed 80 percent of your maximum heart rate (subtract your age from 220 to estimate your maximum heart rate).

Ellen Van Maris

In addition to helping you maintain perfect health and fitness, aerobic exercise, as we stated earlier, also may contribute to maintaining low body-fat levels. It is an important adjunct to your weight training, but do not practice it any more than two or three times weekly if you are trying to gain weight. Four or five aerobic workouts each week are fine if you are not trying to increase muscle size. And if you are trying to get rid of body fat, you may want to push yourself to a temporary peak, practicing aerobics six days a week.

If you chose to train every other day, you would .be training four times one week and three times the next. The standard answer to the question of training frequence is to train each body part at least twice and no more than three times weekly.

Beginners are usually advised to train their whole body in one workout, three times weekly: for instance, Monday, Wednesday, and

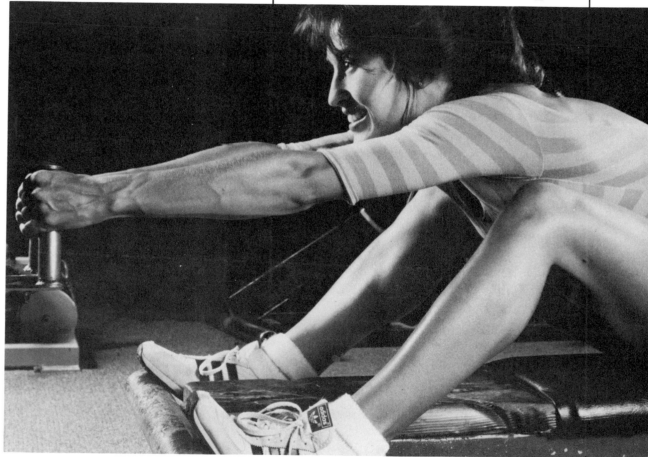

A seated pulley row is performed by Rachel McLish.

Workout Frequency

There is always controversy about how many times a week you should train. Actually, it varies according to your level of experience, your tolerance to vigorous exercise, and your ability to recuperate after workouts.

To start with, why lock yourself into training a certain number of times each week?

Friday. (A day's rest from the weights following your workout day is recommended.)

There are, of course, several other combinations possible while still scheduling a rest day after each workout.

The other alternative, especially if you have been training for a few months, is to split your routine, performing the first half one day

Lisa Kolakowski

and the second half the next day. This could translate as training your chest, back, and arms one day, and shoulders, legs, and abdominals the next. You may still take a complete rest day after each workout (known as the every-other-day split) or you can work out two days in a row and rest on the third day, then work out another two days and rest the following day, and so on.

Some very experienced women work out even more frequently than this, training *three days on, one day off*.

The ultimate choice of training frequency is basically dependent upon how often you can train without overloading your muscles. An overtrained body will have a stringy, flat appearance, and you will come to resent your workouts, as enthusiasm wanes and progress drags to a standstill.

Exercise Performance

The way you perform an exercise is important for your physical safety and serves to keep your muscles in good condition. Actually, most women have a natural aptitude for good exercise style, unlike the men who often forsake good style in the quest to lift additional weight.

The golden rule for beginners is to start with light weights, and build up gradually. No two people use exactly the same poundage in all their exercises. You are the best judge of the amount of weight to use for each movement. Stay well within your strength ability.

You should never be so engrossed in lifting a weight that you bend backwards, twist to one side, lift your hips, or swing your body. These are all "cheating" movements, which may help you complete a repetition, but you are only succeeding in cheating your muscles out of their proper exercise.

A curl, for example, is for the arms. When you swing your body back and forth to rock the weight up you are relieving the arms of direct stress, because the back and legs are aiding in the lift. For the moment, as a begin-

ner, you are urged to keep your exercise style strict. Each movement at this stage should involve a complete contraction and extension of the muscles being exercised. Lock your elbows on presses, rows, and arm exercises. Raise completely up and down on toe raises, thigh extensions, and thigh curls.

Take pride in making each exercise work your muscles over their fullest range. Think about what you look like as you work out. Use a mirror so that you can raise the bar evenly (horizontal). Constantly check that dumbbells are lifted to the same height, that your body does not twist and contort itself in an effort to get the weight up. Perfect exercise style can lead to a perfect physique.

When to Train

Exactly when to train is usually up to the individual's personal timetable. It's a matter of when you can best fit your training in with your work and family commitments. There is some evidence to show that women over 35 have more energy in the early morning, whereas younger women have peak energy in the early evening.

The important thing (although not absolutely essential) is that you try and work out at the same time each day. This will tend to set your internal clock and prepare you for regular training. After a few weeks your body will actually start to look forward to your workouts. As your training time approaches your body will *energize* itself, in anticipation of the accustomed training.

At this moment you may be totally gung ho on bodybuilding. If you are, then we are all for you. We want you to succeed. But over-enthusiasm can be your enemy. Being too enthusiastic too early can wipe you out. The prevailing advice in this chapter on getting started is to take it easy at first. Hold back on what may be a natural temptation to give it your all. Do the exercises correctly, using the proper style and amount of weight for perfect form.

Flexibility — Stretching It Out

Flexibility is the limberness of joints and muscles that permits a maximum degree of movement. It is made possible by the regular practice of stretching exercises. Stretching is an excellent way of warming up the muscles prior to training, and keeping your body joints, tendons, and muscles flexible is very satisfying in itself.

Weight training builds up the muscle and tendon strength, but barbell and dumbbell work only minimally increases the suppleness of joints, muscles, or tendons. Stretching helps keep the joints loose and allows for a complete range of mobility. Muscles can also benefit from being stretched within the limits of their natural boundaries. Tendons shrink if not regularly put to the test and kept in shape.

Although certain movements using barbells increase your flexibility, it is less time consuming to perform your mobility work *without* equipment. Try to do three five-minute workouts a week for attaining ultimate flexibility. You can do these exercises any time, whether on your regular workout days or not. They are not tiring or particularly difficult.

Alternate Thigh Stretch

This exercise will stretch the inner thigh and help firm up the entire buttocks area, while stretching hamstrings (backs of the legs) and all of the back.

Sit on the floor with your back straight, your right leg fully extended, with your foot upright and flexed. Flexing the entire right leg, place the sole of the left foot alongside the inner right thigh and place your hands gently just below the knee of your right leg, one on top of the other.

Take a deep breath, then exhale and bend forward and run your hands down your leg towards your toes. Reach down as far as possible without straining. Inhale and return to the first position. After performing 10 repetitions, repeat the same movement with the left leg extended. Try to keep your back straight and the extended leg tense, with your foot upright and your toes flexed.

Swan Lift

This exercise will stretch almost the entire body, with an additional emphasis on strengthening the lower back, shaping and toning the midsection, and general flexibility.

Lie on your stomach (on a pad or a comfortable carpet). Clasp your ankles, keeping your head up, eyes forward. Inhale and pull on your ankles while lifting and arching your legs and back simultaneously. Exhale and slowly return to the starting position. It is very important to relax in a slow, controlled manner. Try to pull your ankles and arch your back as high as possible, but without straining. Do 10 reps slowly and completely.

Rachel McLish combines a variety of flexibility stretches with her regular workouts.

Spinal Stretch

Here is a really great flexibility movement that works the entire back area, while also stretching the leg hamstring region.

Stand with your feet about 12 inches (30 cm) apart and knees slightly bent, clasping your hands behind your back while bending the torso slightly backwards. Slowly straighten and continue to bend forward until your torso is at a 45 degree angle to your legs. Pull your arms gently up over your shoulders. Return to the starting position and repeat. Exhale as your arms come up over the shoulder position and inhale as you return to the upright position. Perform the movement as effectively as possible and be sure to keep your stomach in and arms high. Also make a conscious effort to tighten your buttocks as you return to the standing position—this is an excellent way to firm them. Perform 12 repetitions.

Whenever you perform stretching exercises it is important that you do not bounce yourself into the stretched position. The idea is to stretch out, *gradually* making demands on your joints, ligaments, and muscles, but not subjecting them to traumatic jolts by bouncing the body up and down. Regular stretching can actually help prevent injuries because you are strengthening the vulnerable areas (injuries as a result of overextension in weight training are common), but do not expect to get overnight results. Research has shown that significant results do not make themselves evident for at least 3–6 weeks after commencement of a stretching program.

Stretching before training is a good idea and fits in well with rope jumping and calisthenics, but do not neglect the importance of stretching *after* your workout . . . if you have time. It promotes even more flexibility because a warm muscle responds better to the stretching effect; it also serves to warm *down* the body, something physiologists believe is just as important as warming up.

Gladys Portugues does a lyrical pose.

Pre-Exercise Warm-up

As well as stretching and rope jumping, you should make a point of warming up for each exercise you do. This simply means that the first set of each exercise should be done with about half the regular weight and twice as many reps. This will help to prevent any muscle injury that could occur if you immediately start with a heavy set of exercise without previously warming up.

Older people may find that more than one warm-up set is needed, especially on heavy exercises like squats, deadlifts, and bench presses. If you are troubled by weak knees, then you should warm up your legs with several sets of each exercise prior to using maximum-intensity training.

By taking the time to stretch and warm up properly before and after a workout, your body will perform better and recover from strenuous exercise more effectively.

33

SETS AND REPS

Rachel McLish puts everything into exercise routines.

Doing the Right Amount

In bodybuilding, it is readily acknowledged that there are a thousand and one ways to train, but the important fact to bear in mind is that training without any type of plan at all is *not* one of them. Do you want success? Then plan for it.

Sets and reps are the heart and core of bodybuilding. They are what your workout consists of. When you consider that the amount of sets, reps, and exercises can vary in number to a large degree, and that the myriad possible combinations could reach the hundreds of thousands well, it can all seem very complicated. Everyone wants to know how many exercises they should do and how many sets and reps per exercise.

Conceivably, you could follow an abbreviated routine of just two or three exercises, or you could use a routine of a hundred exercises. The amount of sets you do for each exercise could be anything from one to 50. The number of reps can run the entire range from one to several hundred. Is it any wonder that no two routines are identical? Even training partners performing *totally* similar programs do different amounts of sets and reps.

Even though there are almost as many routines as there are stars in the heavens, people are still intrigued by the idea of finding a perfect routine for themselves. They also have a fixation about knowing the routines of the champs, in the hope that duplicating them will create a similar type of prize-winning physique.

It's worth saying here and now, to give you peace of mind. Following Rachel McLish's routine will *not* give you a body like Rachel's. Exercises, sets, and reps may be the same, but their *effect* on an individual's body is governed by that person's leverage and physiological characteristics, not to mention exercise style, genetic aptitude, and nutrition habits.

When dealing with sets and reps, keep in mind that your routine evolves, and continually changes. If you are training correctly, no two workouts will be the same. Changes, small and large, are a very real part of each workout. Do *not* make the common mistake of thinking that there exists a magic routine for you, which will transform you into an instant Ms. Olympia. Such a routine is not to be found.

But that does not mean you shouldn't start somewhere. You must develop a good routine as a base from which to work. The important point is that any new routine should understress the body rather than overstress it. This will keep injuries to a minimum.

Candy Csencsits loads up with a heavy weight for the squat exercise.

As you get used to the movements you can really "go to it" as your workouts progress.

There are some basic formulas for you to keep in mind as you devise your exercises. It is true that sets of low reps (1–5) will contribute greatly to increased strength. Medium reps (6–10) will build muscle size. High reps (11–20) will build corpuscle size and overall

Bear in mind that there is no magic formula. There is *no* system to be discovered that will get your muscles to click into place and give you a super-looking physique overnight. To repeat our earlier statement: Your routine, whether you are a beginner, an intermediate, or an advanced bodybuilder, is an *evolving* structure. It should change fre-

Kay Baxter does a seated bent-knee raise for her abdominals.

conditioning. High reps will not define the muscles, which is accomplished by incorporating a calorie-reduced nutrition program in conjunction with training.

The following are some general figures to give you an idea of how many sets and reps women perform in various categories of experience.

quently to accommodate the advances made by your body.

Beginners

As we said earlier, beginners should start with light, *easy* weights and perform only one set of 8–12 repetitions per exercise. Never strain or take on more than you can comfortably handle. After two weeks you can graduate to two sets of 8–12 reps. Continue with this for the first few months.

Intermediates

After four to six months of training, your body has been sufficiently immersed in regular workouts for you to increase the number there is a point of no return. In other words, *more* sets and reps are not necessarily better. You may find that training on the intermediate level is still beneficial, with the added twist of increasing the *intensity* of each set.

On the other hand, you may want to simply increase the sets until you are performing 5–6 sets per exercise. Advanced trainers have

The thigh extension is demonstrated by Lori Bowen-Rice.

of sets and poundages even more. At this stage 3–4 sets per exercise is considered about average. Keep the reps between 8–12.

Advanced Trainers

Here's where we get rid of the rules. Generally, advanced women have to subject their muscles to more work than intermediates, but several alternative routes to take (and rules to break if they are so inclined). You can, of course, keep to 3 sets per exercise and increase the number of *exercises*. Or you may vary the number of sets per exercise in order to work on an underdeveloped area (add more sets) or go easy on a well-developed area (do less sets).

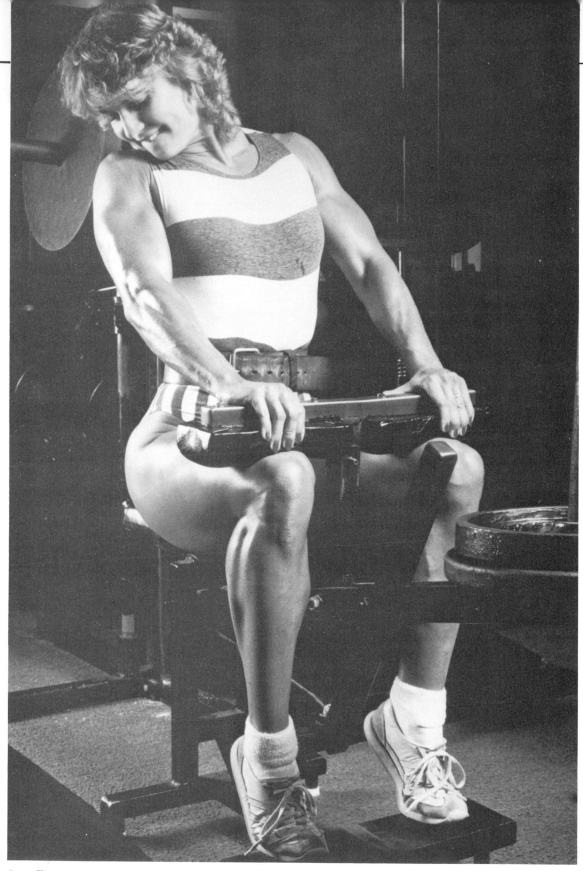

Cory Everson maxes out with a seated calf raise.

The question of repetitions is also subject to variation depending on which muscle group you are exercising. As an advanced trainer you will find out that your thighs will respond best to a system of 10–15 reps. Your calves, abdominals, and forearms may require 15–20 reps per set, while your upper body muscles may thrive best on 8–12 reps.

The above suggestions are not meant to be bodybuilding law, but they are indicative of what women have generally found to be the most useful. Until you find out more about your own body, follow the findings of those who know!

Training Style and Pace

Training style, as we explained earlier, prevents the likelihood of injury if you follow good form. However, good exercise performance can also greatly benefit your development. Yes, there are exceptions.

What is good exercise performance? It is the lifting of a weight from start to finish of the exercise in a smooth manner, using only the muscles directly involved in the lift. You cannot bend the knees and throw a weight up.

Mary Roberts takes a wide grip for lat-machine pulldowns.

You cannot bounce the bar on your body to give it momentum.

Let us take the curl as an example. A perfect curl starts with the bar held in front of the thighs, with straight, *locked* arms and legs. The bar is then curled (raised) by only moving the forearms. The upper arm is held vertically against the side. The trunk (upper body) remains vertical throughout.

Contrast a *strict* curl with a *cheat* curl. When you perform a cheat curl (loose style) you will start with the arms slightly bent, the torso leaning forward, and the knees bent. As you begin the curl you thrust your knees backwards, lean your torso forward, and rock your torso back to aid in the curling action.

In the early stages of bodybuilding, all your exercises should be done in very strict style. Later, as you learn about how your body reacts to various exercises and their performance, you may find it advantageous to cheat during the last few reps on some exercises, when you find that you just cannot perform any more strict repetitions.

There are, however, three cheating movements which you should *never* do:

1. When performing the preacher curl, never "drop" the weight as the arm straightens in the low position. This will cause catastrophic tendon or biceps injury. Lower the weight under complete (slow) control for every repetition.
2. During the bench-pressing exercise, *never* bounce the bar on your breastbone (sternum) in order to help the weight upwards. You can badly bruise or even crack your rib cage.
3. When squatting, *never* bounce your thighs against your lower legs in the low part of the exercise. This is just too hard on the knees and will eventually cause injury.

There is a golden rule about exercise performance that is paramount. It is simply that you should use the exercise style that

An upright row for the shoulders is done Carla Dunlap-style.

A cross-bench pullover for the chest muscles is performed by Carolyn Cheshire.

will best *fully* stimulate your muscles. This means that for the most part your exercises should be performed strictly, using a full range of motion, exercising in a rhythmic and smooth fashion. But at the same time, there is merit in occasionally using loose form in some exercises. We call this *controlled creative cheating.*

Let's look at the curl again as an example. Assume that you are in the middle of a set. You have done five very strict curls but you cannot do another one. You have the option of putting the weight down (and not getting the full benefit of 8–10 reps) or you can loosen up your style and continue. It is usually better to continue, because even though in cheating the curl *upwards* you take much of the effect away from the biceps, you can still maximally stress the muscle as you *lower* the weight slowly (known as the negative effect).

Never forget that healthy muscles adapt very quickly to strict exercise. You do need to change training style, sets, reps, and exercises fairly frequently. Strict, high-intensity quality training, however, should form the basis of your workout. Controlled cheating is to be used on occasion when your exercises would benefit from this particular style. Moderation is the key here. If you cheat in each exercise, you will get nowhere fast.

Training pace is the rate at which you progress through your routine. It is more important than you may think. Firstly, how quickly should you execute your repetitions? Actually, there is not a great deal of heated argument over this question, because successful bodybuilders seem to find that both methods work equally well. Certainly, the beginner should not try to exercise quickly. The "groove" (the path the weight travels in each exercise) has to be established before you can do speed reps. And again, if you are using really heavy weights for low reps, it is not advised to work quickly at all. As time goes on and you know how to *feel* your exercises as you lift the resistance, you can work at a faster rate, if you want to complete your workout sooner.

It is important to rest between your sets and exercises. You should start the next set when your breathing returns to normal. This advice isn't always suitable, because some trainers have interpreted it as resting for up to ten minutes between each set.

It is true that the less you rest between each group of repetitions, the more stress you

Dinah Anderson shows good form in a gym workout.

place on the muscles, but it is not always true that more is better. If you train *too* rapidly, you will *outrun* your cardiovascular system. In other words, you will be benefitting your heart and lungs at the expense of your muscles. The oxygen debt, deep breathing, and accompanying discomfort will hold you back from doing justice to the muscles being trained.

On the other hand, training slowly with long (5–10 minute) rests between sets will cause your energy level to drop. You could even find yourself yawning.

Although it may take you a while to get into it, the ideal rest period between each set is 60–80 seconds. You will need to rest a little more between heavy, combination exercises for large muscle groups such as squats, bench presses, rowing, and deadlifts.

Only as a contest approaches will you need to reduce your rest periods below 60 seconds, but this is a time when you are trying to incorporate the cardiovascular effect with high-intensity training in order to maximize your condition (full, hard muscles, with a minimum of body fat). The shape that a bodybuilder gets in before a contest is an extreme condition which is temporary. You do not sustain this ultratightness all year round.

It is now time to impart the good news that you may rest up to a full five minutes between working out particular *body parts.* For example, after working your thighs with various exercises, resting briefly between each, you may subsequently take a break of five minutes or so. The same goes for each body part—arms, shoulders, chest, abs, back. Take a breather before moving on to the next area. This allows the blood (the pump) to stay in the region for a while until you move on to another section. It's the break that refreshes! When you progress to another area of the body, you should get back into the 60–80-second rest between sets.

Finding the right number of sets and reps is an ever-changing process. However, as you perform your routines your body will let you know when the time is right for a change.

The low-pulley lat exercise is performed by Linda Assam.

PSYCHO POWER

Gladys Portugues shows off her biceps in a playful pose.

The Magic of Thinking Big

According to bodybuilding expert Bill Reynolds: "The mind is one of the most awesome and powerful forces on earth. Properly utilized, your mind can help you build one of the greatest bodies in the world."

There is no doubt that the mind can completely control the body's physical reactions to outside stimuli. A positively tuned mind can render a body impervious to heat as evidenced by people who can walk on red-hot coals and not feel pain. It can stimulate the release of adrenaline from the sudden visualization of fear. In Africa, witch doctors, who are believed in with total faith, can either cure or curse believers with nothing more than a chanted spell.

The woman bodybuilder should use her mind to help her in the quest for physical perfection. First and foremost, of course, is to program yourself for success. Your mind is your own personal computer, and it is up to you to program it for success. The brain controls everything we do, and like a computer we can program it with aims, orders, and even enthusiasm.

Regardless of their position in life, all successful people involve themselves in the art of positive thinking. If you do not think you can do something, then you will never be able to succeed. Start now by telling yourself that you are going to develop a great-looking body, and let nothing stop you.

"Most people are their own worst enemies," says top bodybuilder Rachel McLish. "They stand in their own way of progress. The standard cop-out is: 'I could never succeed at that, so I won't even try.'"

You must involve yourself in positive thoughts when you train your body. Success is yours for the taking, but it won't come about from a sloppy attitude towards your workouts. A training routine has to be a serious practice. You can't take time off between sets to read a book or watch television. Don't get in the habit of talking and joking during a workout. Never respond to anyone while you are exercising. Politely tell then not to talk to you while you are training, and they will get the message.

Before every set, tell yourself quietly how many reps you will accomplish with a given weight. This doesn't mean that you go all out for every set you ever do. But you must program your mind, and tune in your concentration for *every* set. It is the positive attitude of constantly programming and concentrating on your goals that builds good neuromuscular efficiency and strong nerve pathways. Your mind-to-muscle relationship improves, all of which adds to your performance level, and ultimately superior results are achieved.

Dr. Lynn Pirie performs an impressive pose to show her excellent arm definition.

The attainment of strength and beauty is the right of every woman. It is something to work for, an ambition to accomplish. Some women have this urge to build a superb body deep within their souls. They hardly need inspiration to train, nor do they need self-belief or motivation. Sometimes, however, this musclemania deserts them. It may be age, or perhaps they become interested in other activities. They still want that dynamite body, but the all-encompassing *need* is not there. They may ask themselves if the work is worth the effort.

It is at such times that you need to summon the power of your mind to program your brain for success. You need to see the light at the end of the tunnel again—remind yourself of your original goals. With enough mental effort, you can remake your body into anything your genetic endowment permits. It's a question of mind over matter!

Heavy weights are required for Kay Baxter's back squats.

The Enthusiasm Factor

Many women assume that if they train with enough enthusiasm, motivation, and intensity, their gains and progress will never cease. This is not even true of men bodybuilders, and it is one of the most erroneous ideas in bodybuilding today.

Too much intensity will cut short your progress faster than anything else. After only a few workouts your body presses the alarm button and nervous exhaustion sets in. The same goes for workouts that are too long in duration, or training frequency that does not allow for sufficient rest. What these practices do, if persisted with, is cause severe overtraining, resulting in inevitable frustration and disillusionment. The fact that many bodybuilders make no improvement in spite of superhard efforts is one of the most visible aspects of training. To get a return of zero from 100 percent commitment is heartbreaking, but it happens all the time.

It is true that stimulation must come from hard training, but this training must be tailored to your condition. Never let your emotions carry you through a workout, trying for records, doubling your efforts, extending your workout time. Unless this advance is made with small progressive steps you are doomed to early failure.

Training too hard, using forced reps in every workout, struggling, and using bad exercise form to hoist heavier and heavier poundages develop from unrealistic bodybuilding expectations. By aspiring so high and wanting to be the best, it is easy for overenthusiasm to take the place of common sense.

While guarding against training too hard or too much, we must not become overly complacent. Progress comes from intelligent training, using prudence and caution. Small steps rather than big leaps are the order of the day.

Your tolerances to exercise varies: Certainly what becomes too much for one woman can be totally inadequate for another. This brings us to the topic of body feedback. The more you learn about your reaction to exercise, the better able you will become at tailoring your workouts to your individual needs. If you feel drained when you are due for your next workout, obviously you are overtraining. Cut back and exercise with more moderation.

What about the people who can't drum up enough enthusiasm? Basically they want success like anyone else. They want a great-looking body, but after a few workouts their interest wanes; their commitment, once so strong, falls away. Enthusiasm comes from wanting. In the early stages of training it goes deeper. You don't just *want* a better body, you *need* it.

If your want has subsided somewhat, you are going to have to drum it up again. Read books on bodybuilding and study the pictures of other top women bodybuilders. Allow yourself to feel the envy. Don't just flick the pages casually. Picture yourself on the pages. Imagine the glory of fame if that's what you want. By admitting this to yourself, you will fire your ambitions, and fuel your desire to the hilt. You don't have to tell the world. It can still be your secret.

Keep up to date on women's bodybuilding. Never miss an issue of *Muscle & Fitness*, *Flex*, *Shape*, or *MuscleMag International*. The variety of points of view will keep you abreast of the latest trends, and the photographs will serve to inspire you to unbelievable achievement.

Watch bodybuilding videotapes. Rachel McLish and other top women bodybuilders have all made training tapes which are on the market. The Ms. Olympia contests are taped and can be purchased through the bodybuilding magazine media.

Go to shows! There are bound to be several NPC (National Physique Committee) contests in your area for amateur bodybuilders. The IFBB (International Federation of Bodybuilders) professional shows are also well worth attending, even if it means travel-

Tina Plakinger knows the meaning of pumping up to the limit.

ling some distance to attend one. You will never forget the excitement of a Ms. Olympia contest. Bodybuilding is your hobby. Decide now to be a part of it in every way.

A lack of inspiration can be overcome in many ways. Try training in a different setting, at a friend's house, or a new commercial gym. Some women bodybuilders find it inspirational to train with a male workout partner. "It stirs up the hormones," said one top woman bodybuilding champ. . . . "I'm not going to give up on a set until it's completed if I know some guy is counting the reps for me."

When you really believe in yourself, or are inspired by some outside force, and completely determined to achieve your goal, your mind releases the amount of energy you need to give it your best shot. And you can't ask for anything more than that!

TOUGHING IT OUT

Shelley Gruwell squeezes out another incline bench press.

The Benefits of Regular Workouts

Perseverance is your key to making it big in bodybuilding. Results come at varying speeds, but they will not come at all if you do not persist with regular workouts.

Claudia Wilbourn, Ms. California, knows all about toughing out the workouts:

Changes sometimes recur so slowly, especially at the beginning, one is surely tempted to quit. Early on in my training I expected instant perfection. I trained my legs and buttocks, because they were my stubborn areas, for five days a week. I did squats, uphill sprints, thigh extensions . . . all to improve symmetry and muscle quality of my legs and hips. I was so discouraged at the slow progress that I hid my legs under leg warmers or sweat pants and just dropped all my heavy leg training. I had given in. A year later I realized my mistake. It is far better to make small strives than none at all. I resumed my leg training, committing myself to a process of steady improvement . . . and I was rewarded with better results than I had had in years. Patience and perseverance had paid off!

The first thing to put into practice is *goal setting*. It will greatly aid your persistence. Do not set impossible goals because failure to reach them can undermine anyone's self-image. Stay within the boundaries of attainable ambition. It's far better to understate a goal and achieve it quickly than to set an impossible task and doom yourself to failure.

Your goal setting with regard to bodybuilding should be in two parts:

1. Write down your long-term goal— reaching certain measurements, winning a particular contest, etc.
2. Write down your interim goals, such as adding 20 pounds to your bench press or increasing your arms to 11 inches.

Keep the list in a highly visible area (on your gym wall). A goal is a commitment to stay on course. Like a rocket headed for the moon, the course has been set. If it strays for a moment, bring it back and reaffirm the correct direction. The critical thing about goal setting is that you allocate yourself a time frame by which each goal is to be met. By committing yourself to bench press 20 pounds more in six weeks, you are increasing the urgency of the promise.

Look at the incredible biceps of Carla Dunlap!

Get physique pictures taken of yourself every year. They will serve to remind you of how far you have come and where you are going. Without regular pictures you will not be fully aware of your condition. Every champion or would-be champion keeps a record of his or her condition in this way. Otherwise you have

A single-arm pulley curl is demonstrated by Shelley Gruwell.

only odd memories that are too vague to fully recall.

It's the same with a training log. You should record your exercises, sets, reps, and poundages for every workout. Georgia Miller-Fudge can go back up to 12 years with a few flicks of the pages! That's pretty handy infor-

mation to have at your fingertips! Not that Georgia goes all out every workout, trying to beat the performance of her last workout. This would soon lead to a burnout situation. A training log should be used to keep you informed about your workouts. You should cycle your training for utmost benefit, planning your workouts to gradually increase in intensity as you aim for a particular peak. And after you reach that peak (such as entering an important competition) you can taper off or "down cycle" your training for a while.

The advantage of a training log is that it allows you to compete with yourself (when you wish to) from one day to another, or one year to another. A training log should record everything—not just your sets, reps, and poundages, but how the workout felt. Were you tired, overheated, drained, or did the sets come easily? Were you full of pep?

When you achieve a new record in a workout, put a star beside the appropriate set. Those stars will indicate your progress. Record your measurements and weight every month or two along with diet changes, minor injuries, and details of what supplements you are taking. It is also important to state whether you cheated during an exercise. You may feel a training log is not necessary; however, it is a useful tool. Most of the better woman bodybuilders keep a record. It helps to maximize your progress.

Are your workouts dragging? You may find that listening to music will help. Current scientific evidence has shown that various kinds of music will help you breeze through a workout that you might otherwise find boring. Certainly aerobic exercise is far easier for virtually everyone if it is performed to music.

Finally, if you come up with a problem that you cannot find an answer to, don't let it drain you. Ask others about how they handled the same problem. Attend seminars, read avidly, and gather as much knowledge as you can about bodybuilding. When you are totally immersed in the iron game your ability to stick with it will be no problem.

Home or Gym Training?

The question of whether you should train at home or in a commercial gym is impossible to answer with authority. Most top women bodybuilders train at commercial gyms. However, it is also true that in their climb to the top most of these same champions spent at least a portion of their training time at home, in the garage or basement, often with only the bare necessities of a barbell set, a bench, and squat racks. Both locations, home and gym, have clearly defined advantages.

Home training is certainly convenient. You can do your workout just when you feel like it. You also have the advantage of total privacy. Reg Park trained in his garage with just one friend as a workout partner, and made the best progress of his life. Christine Zane frequently trains at home, with her husband, as does Anita Columbu with her husband Franco. In fact, most of the top women have some training apparatus at home where they do their workouts for months at a time. They do, however, train extensively in gyms as contest time approaches.

One fact remains: You have to be totally dedicated to working out if you train at home. It's so easy to relax in front of the television, have a glass of wine, some food, and presto!— you become too lazy to get started. Missed workouts become commonplace and before you know it your progress has gone into reverse. This frequently happens to the home trainer. The very convenience of being able to train *any* time you want, becomes a factor in causing missed workouts.

A commercial gym, on the other hand, has a competitive atmosphere. Whether you know it or not, you invariably train harder and faster in a gym where other people are exercising. There may, of course, be times when your car breaks down, or the weather is against you, but few experienced bodybuilders deny that taking your workouts at a good gym is the faster way to reach your goal.

Factors against the commercial training setup are the possibilities of overcrowding. (There's hardly going to be a line up for the squat racks in your basement gym.) Monday nights are often impossible at popular commercial establishments, because many body-

Debbie Duncanson gets into a dumbbell curl exercise.

builders take both Saturdays and Sundays off from their training and almost everyone is anxious to work out on the first day of the week.

Women who are excessively shy may like the refuge of training at home in seclusion, but always remember . . . however skinny or

Candy Csencsits shows strict form in the seated pulley row.

fat you are, there are always people in worse shape. Besides, no one will be looking at you anyway. The members are invariably far too busy trying to catch sight of themselves in the mirrors than to be critically analyzing you.

For the most part, temperature will be balanced in a commercial gym (you may not have air conditioning at home). Then there's the variety of equipment. Although it has been established that barbells and dumbbells can be effective on their own, a variety of apparatus, pulleys, leg machines, etc., can prove to be a valuable contribution to the ultimate success of your bodybuilding endeavors.

There will be a greater variety of fixed dumbbells and barbells at a commercial gym. This alone will save you the somewhat tedious job of changing plates every time you want to alter poundages. The luxury of fixed dumbbells, set out in rows, graduating in 5-lb. increments, is hard to beat.

Before joining a gym, find out exactly what you get for your money. You may find that the basic annual fee doesn't entitle you to the use of all the facilities, or even all the apparatus. Also consider the distance you will have to travel to reach the gym. Would winter weather prove a problem on the route? Would travel to and from the gym take too much of your valuable time?

And then there's the fact that, unlike your home gym, a commercial gym is seldom open 24 hours a day, seven days a week! You should also determine whether your gym membership includes personal instruction. This is very important to some people. Others, who feel that they know what they are doing, may resent an instructor telling them what to do. There's a point to be considered here. Some establishments insist that you exercise in the style that they dictate. If you are an experienced bodybuilder, this may rub you the wrong way. Check out the gym's policy before joining.

Most gym establishments today are honorable and reliable. In the past, things were not always that way, but the prime concern of any commercial gym is the same as it ever was—to make money. What you should ask yourself is, "Do they give *value* for my money?"

Lori Bowen-Rice uses psycho power.

If a pushy salesperson counters your negative reply with a question (this is a convenient way of drawing you back into a two-way conversation about the establishment), you are quite within your rights in saying politely:

"Look, I don't have to explain or justify myself in *any* way. I have told you I will think about it, and if I decide to join this gym, I will let you know."

The salesperson may be a little taken aback, but he or she will respect you.

How do you know whether you are considering a good or a bad gym? If there are a lot of electrical devices, such as vibrator belts and roller machines, and the salesman insists that these will help you lose pounds, forget it. The main tools for bodyshaping are barbells, dumbbells, treadmill areas, benches, pulleys, and sturdy exercise stations.

A thick pile carpet, soft music, chrome apparatus, and air conditioning are not necessities for a good gym. Rather, look for simple, strong apparatus and, most of all, an enthusiastic group of people training.

If everyone on the gym floor is sitting around talking, chances are you will be doing the same if you join. Look for a busy training area that will inspire you to train hard and progress. The clanging of barbells and dumb-

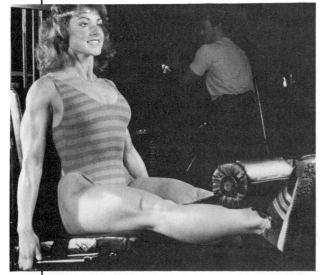

Kike Elomaa works out with leg extensions.

Gladys Portugues demonstrates a hack squat.

bells on the gym floor is the right music for you—not Frank Sinatra singing "My Way" while the gym members sit around the juice bar gossiping.

Check the days that the gym is open. If it caters to men, too, you may only be able to train every other day, which might not suit your schedule. Ideally, a gym should be open to you at least six (preferably seven) days a week. We are not suggesting you train daily, but it's always nice to know that if you have to miss a workout, you can always return the next day.

Gym fees vary greatly. Shop around and compare. Only buy equipment for your home that is made by a well-known company. Do not buy what you are unlikely to use. Once you have made the decision to join a gym or set up your own home training apparatus, remember that it is your *persistence* that is the real consideration. It is the key to your success.

APPARATUS AND AIDS

Sit-ups with gravity boots are performed by Kay Baxter.

Bodybuilding Tools

Name any sport, hobby, or pastime, and you will find a bounty of accessory items that are supposed to make life easier. Bodybuilding is no different. There are numerous aids to help you in the job of building your body.

We are often asked what the minimum requirements are for a woman to start bodybuilding. The answer is that a barbell set, including a pair of dumbbell rods, is absolutely necessary. You should also acquire an exercise bench (preferably one that adjusts easily to an incline) and a pair of squat stands. The barbell set should contain enough discs of free weight to allow for substantial variations of poundage. Certainly nothing less than a 110-pound set is acceptable. That's it! You're in business. Nothing else is needed.

What usually happens, of course, is that as you get into bodybuilding you start to acquire additional training accessories. Admittedly, some are more a luxury than necessity, yet once you get used to them, you may wonder how you ever did without them.

Items such as leg warmers, tights, gloves, and sweatbands may not have a direct bearing on your training progress, yet they can make your workouts more pleasurable. On the other hand, triceps bars, arm blasters, and weight belts are such positive aids that their usefulness is almost beyond debate.

We do not recommend that you spend a lot of money on bodybuilding accessories. What we do advise is not to skimp on the necessities. You need a weight set and a bench, and preferably squat racks. None of these things will ever wear out. They are an investment rather than an expense, and only if you abuse them (leave them outdoors in bad weather) will they lose their value.

As far as other accessories and extras are concerned, whether you acquire them or not is up to you. Many have specific purposes and can prove very helpful. You cannot knock the ultimate usefulness of a weight-support belt (which helps protect your back), or wrist straps (which allow you to do more repetitions), or chalk (which gives you a stronger grip), or gloves (which prevent calluses). This list is endless. If you are really enthusiastic about bodybuilding, then buy the items that you feel will genuinely help your training. Make a decision based on common sense and you will not waste money. In fairness to the manufacturers, most training accessories prove to be a positive help. When you find a training aid that works well and you can afford, use it.

Beginners should not use weights with gravity boots—an injury could result!

Training Aids

Weight-Training Belts

Once you start training with heavier weights, a good-quality weight belt is invaluable. All serious trainers wear a belt, especially for exercises such as deadlifts, rowing, and squats. Some women wear belts throughout their entire workouts, but if you feel uncomfortable with it, you can just use it for certain basic exercises.

Belts are usually made of leather and are available in 4-inch (10-cm) and 6-inch (15-cm) widths (occasionally larger). There is dubious advantage in a woman requiring anything wider than a 4-inch belt. The usefulness of a weight belt is that it helps protect the lower back by giving additional support. It also affords the wearer greater confidence in lifting heavier poundages and contributes in a positive way to increasing strength.

Weightlifting gloves

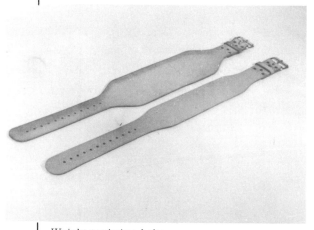

Weight-training belts

Sweatbands

On a hot day, when you are really pushing your training intensity, sweat can trickle from your brow and sting your eyes. A sweatband can prevent this, and also serve to hold your hair away from your face and eyes, permitting full concentration on your exercise performance.

Gloves

The first person to regularly wear training gloves was Serge Nubret of France. The idea didn't catch on quickly, but nowadays most professional bodybuilders wear them. These special half-finger gloves form a barrier between the sweat of your hands and the slippery surface of the bar. They also help you to avoid the development of unsightly calluses on your fingers and palms.

Training Straps

The strength in your grip frequently gives out before the larger muscles used in such exercises as deadlifts, chins, rowing, pulldowns, and shrugs. A set of training straps (one for each hand) can actually enable you to perform several more reps than if straps were not used. More reps means more progress. Training straps are usually made from strong cotton webbing.

Arm blaster

Arm Blasters

The arm blaster is a shaped aluminum strip about 5 inches (12.5 cm) wide and 24 inches (60 cm) long, supported at waist height by a strap placed around your neck. The object of the unit is to brace your elbows in an immobile state while you curl barbells and dumbbells or perform triceps pressdowns. It eliminates cheating and fosters a very strict exercise style. Arm blasters are gaining in popularity among serious women bodybuilders.

E-Z Curl Bars

If you relax your arms by your sides, you will observe that your palms tend to face towards the body. Cambered bars, or E-Z curl bars, were designed to allow for a more comfortable grip. The original idea was to make the curling exercise more *natural*. But now, about 50 years after their invention, E-Z curl bars are not only used for a variety of curls, including preacher bench curls and reverse curls, they are also widely used in close-grip bench pressing and the overhead triceps stretch—with a difference. Instead of placing your hands on the angled hand grip areas, grip the center of the bar over the gentle curve where you can get a firm hold. E-Z curl bars are not superior to straight bars for curling, but they exercise different sets of muscle fibres. Many bodybuilders who return to the use of a straight curling bar find it as stimulating as their original change from straight to cambered.

Chalk

Many bodybuilders, powerlifters, and all weightlifters "chalk up" before attempting demanding sets. Chalk can be very useful to bodybuilders, especially in warm climates where the palms are prone to sweating profusely. Chalk can definitely help you hold onto that bar when your hands are prone to slipping outwards or your fingers are unable to maintain a grip.

Head Straps

Usually made from leather, nylon, or acrylic, head straps are designed to offer resistance for direct neck work. The strap itself fits comfortably around the neck and extra weight discs can be attached accordingly. Most exercises involve the neck to some degree and only those women with underdeveloped necks or those with sagging chin muscles require specialized work in this area.

Heel Boards

The majority of men and women feel uncomfortable squatting with a weight if their feet are flat on the ground. A heel board (merely a piece of wood 2½ inches × 5 inches × 15 inches) is ideal for placing under the heels to enable good squatting form, as well as lessening the likelihood of strain to the Achilles tendons, the soleus, and upper calf muscles. Heel boards are not manufactured. You have to get them at a lumberyard.

Dipping Belts

If you reach the point when you need more weight (attached to the body) for exercises such as parallel bar dips and chins, or even calf work, then a dipping belt is indispensable. Weight discs are threaded onto a chain (or a dumbbell can be cradled on the chain) and the belt, worn around the waist, gives the body additional resistance.

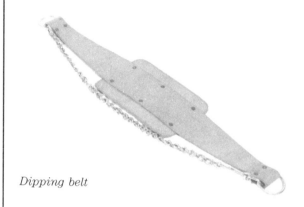

Dipping belt

Ankle and Wrist Weights

Primarily used for aerobic exercise, ankle and wrist weights add resistance to help you break into a sweat earlier and accordingly benefit the heart and lungs to a greater degree. Be sure that you buy these items only if they are fully adjustable and can be fitted snugly to your limbs. Ankle and wrist weights have a positive application when used for straight leg lifts in various angles, but their application as far as progressive resistance is concerned is limited to small increments.

Ankle weights

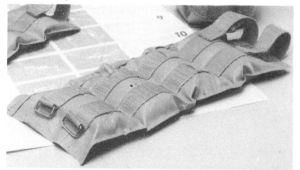

Lat Machines

The general idea of this machine involves a pulley system of weight resistance. Accordingly, lat machines are ideal for pulldowns with a variety of grips and pressdowns, an excellent movement for the triceps. Many lat machines are also fitted with extra pulley wheels to redirect the basic resistance and allow for a greater variety of movements.

Leg Warmers

Originally used exclusively by ballet dancers, leg warmers are now considered virtually indispensable workout accessories. They are usually made of Orlon, acrylic, plastic fiber, or nylon and their function is to insulate the necessary heat to maintain muscle elasticity.

Natural fibres such as wool or cotton have the additional benefits of allowing maximum ventilation on warm days. In really chilly temperatures, try layering a pair of wool or cotton warmers over a pair of synthetic ones for super insulation that still allows moisture evaporation.

E-Z-on collars

E-Z-On Collars

These unique items are used for the instant changing of plates. They do away with standard barbell collars, screws, and wrenches, yet are not recommended for use with heavy dumbbells. They fit all standard bars.

Gravity Boots

These are boots or clamps that attach to the ankles to enable the wearer to hang upside down. The concept was invented many years ago but only comparatively recently were special boots marketed. Their primary function is to relieve the sensation of spinal deterioration, stretching the spine out and reversing the gravitational pull. A variety of twists and sit-ups can be performed in the inverted position, but it is not safe for beginners to use weights with gravity boots.

midsection area. Waist shapers are also available in longline and overall torso models, which increase the sweat areas of the body. They are soft and comfortable and wash instantly in plain water.

Pec-Decks

This apparatus was invented to improve upon the supine flye motion with dumbbells. Something that allowed more comfort was needed (we don't know who invented the unit, but writer/photographer Denie thought

Waist shaper

Waist Shapers

Usually made from a neoprene rubber with a stretchable backing of material, the waist shaper is worn around the midsection. The heat retained promotes perspiration, which constitutes a loss of fluids from the

up the name). The Pec-Deck is used in an upright seated position, with the arms initially straight out to the sides or bent upwards. The movement involves the forward motion of the arms, which places the stress exclusively on the pectoral muscles.

Squatting Belts

Do not confuse these with leather weight belts. A squatting belt is usually made from strong, elasticized material, about 12 inches (30 cm) wide, and fits around the midsection. The idea is to offer greater waistline support, not just around the back, but also the front of the midsection. Squatting belts can actually prevent the stomach from stretching out, which can occur from repeated heavy squatting. They add overall confidence and should be worn in addition to regular leather training belts.

Multi-Purpose Benches

These benches are made in a variety of sizes and are available in all price ranges. The idea is to incorporate as many features as possible into one bench, to accommodate the needs of trainers who do not have a great deal of room for equipment in their homes. Most multi-purpose benches include an adjustable incline bench, leg-curl and thigh-extension attachments, weight stands, and flat-bench facilities. More expensive models include preacher benches, squat stands, dip bars, and even lat-machine attachments.

Multi-purpose bench

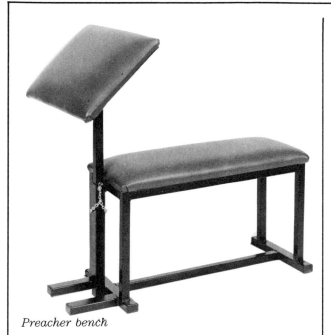
Preacher bench

Preacher Benches

This is a special bench designed to keep the upper arms stationary and at an angle while the trainer curls with either a pair of dumbbells or a barbell. Preacher benches can be used in a standing or seated position, and in most cases the angle of the padded bench surface is adjustable from 30 to 90 degrees.

Crossover Pulley Machines

This cumbersome machine is not considered a home unit because of its size. It enables the trainer to work the upper, middle, or lower pectoral muscles by simply raising or lowering the arms. Crossover pulley machines also work the chest over its fullest range, especially contributing to pectoral striations.

T-Bar Row Apparatus

This unit is designed to take some of the strain and injury potential from the lower back, a common possibility with regular barbell rowing exercises. T-bar rowing units allow for large weights to be used in relative comfort.

Power Racks

Power racks offer a way to train with heavy weights with utmost safety. They are popular in most gyms because they offer protection to the members, especially heavy-training individuals. Power racks are usually made from tough steel tubing with solid steel support pins, which serve to hold a loaded barbell in a horizontal position at varying heights. Many individual trainers are equipping their home gyms with power racks.

Kettlebells

Kettlebells have been around for scores of years, but that's no reason to neglect their usefulness. The primary, and admittedly limited, function of the kettlebell handle is to relieve the wrist of unnecessary strain, particularly in the performance of lateral and forward raises used in deltoid training. If problem wrists are one of your dilemmas, then a pair of kettlebell handles may be your salvation.

Thigh-Extension/Leg-Curl Benches

A very popular apparatus, because almost everyone is looking for a substitute for squats. The thigh-extension/leg-curl bench incorporates a high table surface with a roller bar attachment which enables you to mobilize the leg muscles from both prone and supine positions.

Thigh-extension bench

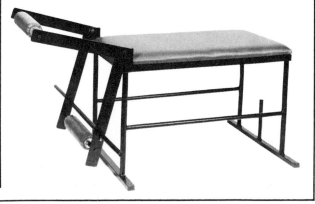

GOOD NUTRITION

Mary Roberts

Food for Thought

If you want to improve your physical appearance, whether you want to build up muscle or lose overall weight, you simply must eat good-quality food. This does not mean you have to spend a fortune on your food intake. Actually, junk foods are often among the most expensive, so if you have been eating it, you can look forward to spending less for nutritious food.

It is the cumulative effect of poor-quality (junk) food that will do you damage. An occasional ice cream or a piece of pie is not going

Cory Everson

Shelley Gruwell

to ruin your body. On the other hand, if you look at children or adults who have been raised on chocolate cake, potato chips, ice cream, candies, and other synthetic junk food, not only will you see an overweight person, but the fat itself will have a "spongy," unhealthy look to it. And the additional side effect of such an unbalanced diet is poor health. Such individuals often have colds, headaches, sinus problems . . . and generally feel run down. After years of poor nutrition, of course, minor ills turn into major sicknesses. Your body has no resistance and more serious, even life-threatening problems may occur.

You can avoid these problems by eating good, wholesome foods. The body's nutritional needs are met by the basic food groups—the grains, meats, fruits and vegetables, and dairy products.

Balanced nutrition requires that you have quantities of each of the basic food groups every day. This is the ideal, but the human body is adaptable and can make up for meals of insufficient nutrients. Your system is constantly compensating for its food intake, so short-term malnutrition is not a problem. However, a continued shortage of essential nourishment will set back your training progress and eventually cause health problems.

A basic standard of good nutritional balance is:

- Fat: 30 percent (saturated fats, 10 percent; unsaturated fats, 20 percent)
- Protein: 14 percent
- Carbohydrates: 56 percent (complex carbohydrates, 43 percent; refined sugar, 14 percent)

Good nutrition constitutes those foods which are nearest to how nature created them. Fruits, vegetables, meats, fish, eggs, milk, cheese, nuts, poultry, and whole-grain products are the good foods. The bad ones include artificially colored and flavored canned foods, deep-fried products, fatty gravies, devitalized white bread and doughnuts, burgers, hot dogs, cakes, candies, cookies, pastries, smoked meat, packaged ham, synthetic sausages, potato chips, crackers, sugary breakfast cereals, pretzels, among others. Avoid precooked, canned, preserved, and packaged foods whenever possible.

It is always best to base your diet on fresh, broiled meats and fish, whole-wheat bread, boiled or poached eggs, unsalted nuts, steamed or raw vegetables (do not boil them). Don't remove the peels from fruits: they contain nutrients that the inside fruit itself does not. Always, however, wash fruits and vegetables thoroughly before eating them raw. They may have been sprayed with harmful pesticides.

Our muscles are about 80 percent water and 20 percent protein. Taking in large quantities of either (or both) will not greatly benefit the woman bodybuilder. Even if you have a strong desire to gain lean body mass (muscle), the body can only assimilate a certain amount at one time. Remember that before protein can be used by the body a stimulus (a hard workout) has to create an urgent need for it.

Yes, protein is important. You should eat about 15–20 grams at every meal. The once popular protein-overload theory has lost a great deal of its credibility. Today it is generally accepted that a woman bodybuilder who exercises regularly and vigorously *does* need a protein intake above the requirements of a nontraining woman. But she doesn't need *huge* amounts.

What are the high protein foods? Milk, eggs, poultry, fish, cheese, nuts, beans, meats, yogurt are all good sources of protein. Eggs are actually the highest-quality protein known. Milk is a close second. Animal proteins are of higher (and more usable) quality than vegetable proteins.

If you are trying to gain muscle size, you probably require additional food. It is important that you eat frequently. Five or six small meals are definitely more beneficial to three large gastronomical extravaganzas. Small meals (snacks) maintain your blood-sugar level on an even keel, prevent excessive hunger and that after-meal gorged feeling that comes from overstuffing yourself. The body will take what it requires and stores the balance as reserve energy.

If you have a high metabolism (the rate at which the body burns fuel while resting), then you will certainly need to eat more than others with a slower metabolism. Gladys Portugues is an example of a woman bodybuilder with a very high (fast) metabolic rate. She really does have to eat every two or three hours, otherwise she loses muscle size.

If you burn up 2,500 calories in a day, then you must eat more than 2,500 calories (via a balanced food intake) in order to gain muscle size. Some women need as much as 3,500 calories daily. If they eat more than that, they will tend to gain weight. If they eat less than that, they will lose weight. The art is to find out by trial and error how many calories you need to gain (or lose) weight slowly.

Although adding or reducing overall caloric intake is the key to gaining or losing weight, food should never be evaluated solely by its calories. Dr. Jean Mayer of the Harvard School of Nutrition says: "A proper diet must provide all the necessary nutrients in sufficient amounts, be palatable, easily available from the viewpoints of economics and convenience, and be balanced in calories to produce the desired calorie deficit for weight loss or additional storage for weight gain."

The underlying urgency is that the food you eat must be of high quality. You simply *must* cut out (or reduce to a bare minimum) calorie-dense foods—unforgivable concoctions prepared or manufactured to appease the whims of taste with no regard for balanced nutrition. Calorie-dense foods are junk foods, characterized by a preponderance of chemical additives, coloring, and preservatives—not to mention their high levels of salt and sugar. (Both are found naturally and abundantly in fruits and vegetables.)

It took the *F-Plan Diet* book to remind us all about the importance of fibre. High-fibre

Gladys Portugues

foods are the exact opposite of calorie-dense foods. They are relatively low in calories, because fibre itself contains very few calories, yet it helps to satisfy your hunger. Actually, if high-fibre foods are eaten in conjunction with other foods, they may even hold back some of the calorie absorption of the other foods. The more you keep to high-fibre nutrients, the less likelihood there is for you to be obese. Fibre foods include whole grains, fresh fruits, bran, and fresh vegetables.

Bread and potatoes, often made out to be the villains when it comes to nutritional talk, are really very good for you and should be eaten every day. Just make sure that the bread doesn't have a lot of added sugar, salt, and preservatives—and certainly don't cover it with calorie-dense butter or sugar-loaded jams, jellies, or marmalades. The same goes for potatoes. Bake or steam them. But don't turn good into bad by frying them or covering them with globs of sour cream or butter.

You should drink some milk every day— at least a small amount. It's true that some people just cannot properly digest milk because of lactose intolerance. These people can add the enzyme lactase to their milk (various brand names are available at pharmacies and drugstores). Milk is high in calcium, the important ingredient for bone strength. Calcium also helps muscles contract. Should your body not be fully supplied with adequate calcium, it will rob your bones or teeth for its supply (2–3 glasses of milk per day are recommended). There are, of course, other foods high in calcium. They include cheddar cheese, yogurt, dried beans, almonds, brazil nuts, and leafy vegetables (collards, broccoli, cabbage, kale, spinach).

Unfortunately, most of us love to cover our foods with salt (sodium chloride). But nature has already put salt in our foods. There is ample in most fruits and vegetables. Not only do we add salt when we eat our meals, but invariably the food companies have already overloaded their products with salt in the first place. A Big Mac contains 1,510 milligrams of sodium; even cottage cheese, a popular bodybuilder's food, contains 850 milligrams of sodium in just one cup.

As well as the health hazards of sodium there is also a specific problem for the bodybuilder: *One part of sodium holds 180 parts of water.* Many women have followed all the rules of contest preparation, calorie reduction, and training only to forget about the necessity of sodium reduction. Accordingly, they enter a contest looking somewhat bloated—even waterlogged!

The quality of results you get from your training depends on the quality of food you put into your body. It is the *activator* that brings it all together. If you are training progressively, then your food intake is responsible for the ultimate shape of your body.

Weight Addition and Reduction

Simply put, a pound of muscle contains 600 calories, and a pound of fat contains 3,500. Fat has more calories than muscle because there is more water in muscle than in fat (muscle has 70 percent water, fat has 15 percent).

To stimulate one pound of muscle weight each month, and make a total gain of 12 pounds in a year, you would have to increase your caloric intake by 600 (the number of calories in a pound of muscle), multiplied by 12 (the number of months in a year) or 7,200 calories a year, over and above the amount of calories needed for your actual weight maintenance. To work out how many extra calories you require daily to gain pure muscle at this rate, merely divide 7,200 by 365 (the number of days in a year) and you'll come up with approximately 19 extra calories a day to add a pound of muscle a month. It would, of course, be worthwhile to exceed this amount to ensure you are getting the extra nourishment, but, on the other hand, do not overeat.

Marjo Selin heads the line-up.

There is absolutely no evidence to support the theory that gaining fat helps the task of gaining muscle. There is no advantage in providing your muscles with many times the amount required for growth. You will only gain unwanted fat! This is a mistake that many men make in their quest for size at any cost.

If you think that gaining a pound of muscle a month is not much, then you are not being realistic. Muscle growth is sporadic. You may gain three pounds in one month or only

Bev Francis and Rachel McLish

one pound in three months, but to average 12 pounds in one year is very substantial.

To lose weight, you must restrict your food intake to control the results. Many books have been written on the subject of losing weight. Here are the alternatives to how it can be done:

1. Reduce your caloric intake.
2. Perform daily aerobics.
3. Have your fat removed surgically.
4. Take potentially dangerous thyroid drugs.

Reduce Caloric Intake

The most common method people choose to lose weight is to diet. This method definitely works, but often there is some difficulty in losing the last few pounds of your goal. There may be a problem with loose skin, and invariably the dieter has low energy. Additionally, there are periods when the dieter cannot seem to continue weight loss even with a low-calorie intake.

Daily Aerobics

Aerobics are those exercises that involve any continuous movement. They are often done in conjunction with up-beat music, which stimulates the will to keep going. Aerobics help you to burn calories, shed water (sweat), and generally contribute to fitness, but weight loss will not necessarily be accomplished if you counterbalance your calorie loss by eating more.

Fat Removed

Having your fat removed surgically is painful and not practical for everyone. Fat is usually distributed evenly all over the body. This is definitely not the best way to lose weight. It may fit in with the requirements of a businesswoman or a film star who desires a fast solution to a bulging waistline, or saddlebag thighs, but it is not recommended for bodybuilders.

Thyroid Drugs

Thyroid drugs serve to speed up the metabolic system (the rate at which your body burns up fuel at rest). They have been used by boxers to lose weight and bodybuilders to gain definition. However, these drugs are dangerous, since they can affect your system so violently that you would have difficulty holding a glass of water without spilling it. Thyroid pills assume the role of the thyroid gland in supplying thyroxin, and the gland itself often shuts off its own production of the hormone. Many people who have experimented with these drugs have to take supervised medication to correct the malfunction for the rest of their lives.

Diet and Exercise

A *combination* of diet and exercise is best for bringing about overall weight loss. You are attacking the problem on two fronts—ingesting fewer calories and burning more fuel (calories). If you are excessively overweight, you may want to diet in conjunction with a progressive aerobics program. If you are carrying only a small amount of excess weight, then simply take in fewer calories while maintaining a good bodybuilding program, as described in this book.

When dieting, do not starve yourself. Maintain balanced nutrition and aim to lose only two pounds a week. Trying to lose more will prove unsatisfactory. No one can tell you exactly how many calories to cut back on to reduce weight. The best way is to simply start reducing them systematically. Many women make the mistake of drastically cutting down on food and liquid overnight. This results in an enormous shock to the body, jolting it out of the comfort zone when, in fact, you should be cutting back gradually. Headaches, stomach cramps, and problems with hyperacidity can abound.

There is also something else to bear in mind when dieting. You could find that you

Mae Mollica watches Diana Dennis during a strenuous workout.

lose weight very rapidly during the first few weeks, eating about 2,000 calories per day, but then something happens. You do not continue to lose. This is when your body compensates by effecting a metabolic slowdown. In other words, you do not burn up as many calories at rest as you did before. The answer, of course, is that you will have to burn more calories with exercise or take in even less food.

Meal Plans

The following is a typical meal plan for the average person. It is *NOT RECOMMENDED* for female bodybuilders (or anyone else for that matter!).

UNHEALTHY MENU

Breakfast

	Calories
6 oz. orange juice	90
2 eggs fried in fat	200
2 slices bacon	100
2 slices white toast with butter and jam	330
Meal Total	720

Lunch

Cheeseburger	465
French fries	210
12 oz. cola	145
Meal Total	820

Dinner

Spaghetti with meatballs in tomato sauce	350
¼ loaf Italian bread	300
Tossed salad with dressing	165
8 oz. ice cream	295
Meal Total	1110
Total for the Day	**2650**

Between-meal snacks can easily add another 600–800 calories to this unwholesome menu.

Here are three recommended high-fibre daily menus that constitute a healthy diet for female bodybuilders. They are listed in ascending order according to total daily calories.

MENU 1

Breakfast

	Calories
2 boiled eggs	160
2 slices whole-grain bread	110
¼ small cantaloupe	30
4 oz. plain yogurt	60
Meal Total	360

Lunch

3 oz. canned tuna in a salad with:	170
1 cup steamed green beans	30
1 sliced tomato	35
¼ cup alfalfa sprouts	10
1 tbsp. oil and vinegar	100
1 slice whole-grain bread	55
1 orange	75
Meal Total	475

Mid-Afternoon Snack

1 bran muffin	85
8 oz. skim milk	90

Dinner

4 oz. broiled or roasted chicken	155
½ cup steamed broccoli	25
1 baked potato	90
1 pat butter	50
1 cup diced fresh pineapple	75
Meal Total	395

Evening Snack

¼ cup granola	65
½ cup skim milk	45
Total for the Day	**1515**

MENU 2

Breakfast

	Calories
6 oz. orange juice	90
1 cup oatmeal or rolled oats	130
½ cup fresh strawberries	45
¼ cup milk	40
Meal Total	305

Mid-Morning Snack

1 banana	85
8 oz. skim milk	90

Lunch

2 oz. Swiss cheese	210
2 slices whole-wheat bread	110
Lettuce salad with cucumber and tomato slices	60
Meal Total	380

MENU 3

Breakfast	Calories
6 oz. pineapple juice	95
⅔ cup bran flakes	85
½ cup milk	80
1 poached egg	80
1 slice whole-grain toast	55
Meal Total	395

Mid-Morning Snack

8 oz. fruit-flavored yogurt	260

Lunch

½ cup cottage cheese	120
1 fresh peach, sliced	35
½ cup fresh strawberries	45
1 oz. raisins	80
2 slices crispbread	110
Meal Total	390

Mid-Afternoon Snack

1 bran muffin	85
8 oz. skim milk	90

Dinner

3 oz. cubed lean beef for shish kebab	245
6 cherry tomatoes, 6 mushrooms sliced green pepper	65
Tossed salad with dressing	165
½ cup brown rice	90
Baked apple with 1 tbsp. brown sugar	120
Meal Total	685

Evening Snack

2 oz. raw cashews	200
Total for the Day	**2105**

A nutritionally balanced diet is a vital part of your bodybuilding program. Buy a guide that tells you the calories in foods. Once you learn the basics of healthy eating, you can make substitutions to keep your meal plans interesting. Remember to keep them natural and fresh!

You are indeed what you eat!

Mid-Afternoon Snack

2 oz. raw almonds	200
1 apple	70

Dinner

3 oz. salmon steak	150
broiled with 1 tbsp. oil	125
½ cup brown rice	90
1 halved tomato	35
broiled with 1 tbsp. Parmesan cheese	55
½ cup steamed spinach	25
1 cup fresh fruit salad	80
Meal Total	560

Evening Snack

6 oz. plain yogurt	90
½ cup fresh blueberries	40
Total for the Day	**1815**

THE EXTRA ELEMENT

Candy Csencsits

Supplementation

Food supplementation is required by all those who seek to excel physically or those who wish to enjoy optimal health. It could be argued that in today's stress-filled society, where we have to cope with pollution, noise, and smog, supplementation is necessary for everyone, whether they are athletic or not.

Nutritional experts have ascertained that each vitamin has a RDA (Recommended Daily Allowance), and it is not hard to conclude that those people eating a balanced diet of fresh, natural foods will fill these quotas. However, nutritional research has proven that the RDA allowances are far from adequate, and the daily requirements are substantially higher.

Bodybuilders often have to juggle their diets to effect different changes. As we have discussed earlier, certain foods in varying amounts are needed to increase weight, lose weight, improve definition, and so on. At times, a woman bodybuilder may jeopardize the balance of her diet in order to bring about physical changes. For example, a precontest diet, often commenced three or four months before a show date, can be low enough in calories to prevent adequate nutrition for the body. Under these circumstances it would be wise to offset any possible imbalance by taking a multi-vitamin mineral pill daily.

There is little doubt that a person who is not getting the right amount of nutrition will not be able to function at his or her peak. No one knows this better than the Russians, whose athletes are regularly given hair or blood analysis tests to monitor their nutritional status. Sometimes the athlete is not getting enough iron, or the protein intake is too low. Whatever the case, it is quickly corrected with extra supplementation.

Nutrition books never seem to mention one thing that most of us should know. We should all understand that nutrition *cannot* work miracles. However, correct supplementation of a bodybuilder's diet can put a woman at a tremendous physical advantage. It may be true that more is not necessarily better when it comes to vitamins, but it has to be admitted that *some* is definitely better than *insufficient*!

We are not suggesting that supplementation take the place of wholesome fresh food. You should supplement your food intake with high-quality products to ensure that you are getting enough of what your body needs for top health, strength, condition, and appearance. If you are getting inadequate nutrition, there will be a corresponding decrease

Kay Baxter

in your body's efficiency. The results you are looking for will be less than they could be with maximum nutrition. Although the FDA insists that a balanced diet will provide you with all the vitamins and minerals that you require for optimal health, they may not have the hard-training bodybuilding in mind when they make these pronouncements.

Vitamins

They are found in all foods in varying degrees. Vitamins are not needed to produce energy. They are, in fact, catalysts that "spark" the efficiency and assimilation of other nutrients. Vitamins are essential in varying quantities as links in the metabolism of other nutrients to maintain proficient bodily function. No one food contains all the vitamins necessary for optimal growth and body maintenance (although milk comes close).

Vitamins A, D, E, and K (fat soluble) are not needed daily because they can be stored in the body for short periods. Large dosages could even be harmful, causing diarrhea and nausea. If you want to take high dosages of other vitamins such as the water-soluble B and C vitamins, which *are* needed daily, take them separately to avoid excessive amounts of vitamins A and D.

Vitamin A

For healthy bones, skin, teeth, resistance to infection, and good vision. It is found in fish, eggs, cheese, milk, liver, tomatoes, and carrots.

Vitamin B_1 (Thiamine)

For a healthy nervous system. It is found in pork, organ meats (such as liver, kidney, and heart), whole-grain breads, cereals, peas, nuts, beans, and eggs.

Vitamin B_2 (Riboflavin)

For the metabolism of protein, fats, and carbohydrates for energy and tissue building. It promotes healthy skin, particularly around the mouth, nose, and eyes. It is found in organ meats, liver, sausage, milk, cheese, eggs, whole-grain breads, dried beans, and leafy green vegetables.

Niacin

Promotes a healthy nervous system and skin, aids digestion, and helps cells use oxygen to release energy. It is found in liver, meats, fish, whole-grain breads, dried peas and beans, peanut butter, and nuts.

Vitamin B_6 (Pyridoxine)

Aids in protein utilization and prevention of certain types of anemia. It is also helpful in maintaining normal growth. It is found in liver, kidneys, butter, meats, as well as in fish, cereal, soybeans, tomatoes, peanuts, and corn.

Pantothenic Acid

Helps in the breakdown of fats, proteins, and carbohydrates for energy. It is found in organ meats, egg yolks, meats, fish, soybeans, peanuts, broccoli, cauliflower, potatoes, peas, cabbage, and whole-grain products.

Folic Acid

Promotes the development of red blood cells and the normal metabolism of carbohydrates, proteins, and fats. It is found in organ meats, asparagus, turnips, spinach, kale, broccoli, corn, cabbage, lettuce, potatoes, and nuts.

Vitamin B_{12}

Produces red blood cells in bone marrow and builds new proteins. It helps the normal functioning of nervous tissue. It is found in liver, kidneys, lean meats, fish, hard cheese, and milk.

Vitamin C (Ascorbic Acid)

Helps bond cells together. It produces healthy teeth, gums, and blood vessels and improves iron absorption. It hastens the healing of wounds and resistance to infections. It also aids in the synthesis of hormones that regulate bodily functions. It is found in citrus fruits (grapefruit, oranges, lemons), strawberries, cantaloupes, raw vegetables (especially green peppers), cauliflower, broccoli, kale, tomatoes, potatoes, cabbage, and brussels sprouts.

Vitamin D

Promotes healthy bones and teeth and helps the body absorb calcium and phosphorus. It is found in liver, egg yolks, foods fortified with Vitamin D such as milk; it is also produced in the body by exposure to direct sunlight.

Vitamin E

Protects red blood cells and retards destruction of vitamins A and C. It is found in wheat-germ oil, rice, leafy green vegetables, nuts, margarine, and legumes.

Vitamin K

Permits blood clotting. It is found in spinach, kale, cabbage, cauliflower, and pork liver.

Minerals

Many minerals are required to maintain healthy bones and teeth, such as calcium, while others aid in hormone production. Calcium is also utilized to maintain muscle tone and muscle recuperation after exercise, and it is partially responsible for heartbeat regulation. The other essential minerals include sodium, potassium, chlorine, copper, sulphur, zinc, manganese, and magnesium.

Protein Supplements

Protein is needed to build muscle. In fact, a muscle is 20 percent protein—the rest is water. However, the building blocks within the

Shelley Gruwell shows good form doing incline dumbbell curls.

protein—the amino acids—are most important.

The most recent findings show that 98 percent of the adult population requires no more than .37 grams of protein per pound of bodyweight per day; children and teenagers, pregnant women, nursing mothers, and athletes need slightly more. Women bodybuilders in need of added muscle size could use extra protein, but huge amounts are not required.

There are hundreds of proteins. Each is, in fact, a different combination of amino acids. Twenty-two amino acids have been discovered (identified), all but eight of which can be manufactured by the body itself. These are known as essential amino acids and they must come from food or supplementation.

The interesting fact about proteins is that they can only be used by the body to build muscle if their content of amino acids is balanced correctly. This combination never seems to happen by itself in natural foods, which means no high-protein foods can be fully utilized. The protein in eggs is closest to being complete: Over 90 percent can be used.

Dairy products, fish, meat, and poultry are also high on the list with 60–80 percent of their protein content being usable. Grains, legumes, and vegetables are lower in usable protein, usually between 40–60 percent.

The fundamental function of protein is the maintenance and growth of tissue. If you are not getting enough, you will suffer loss of weight, have diminished resistance to disease, and you will get tired easily. On the other hand, continual large doses of protein over and above your requirements can actually be harmful to the body. It can cause calcium loss, weakening bones, and it can even contribute to kidney problems and gout.

Dr. Lynn Pirie enjoys doing outdoor workouts.

Lori Bowen-Rice

Editor of *Muscle & Fitness* magazine Bill Reynolds is adamant that a hard-training woman bodybuilder needs one gram of high-quality protein per pound of bodyweight each day. His theory is supported by none other than superstar bodybuilder and multi-Olympia-winner Rachel McLish.

There are scores of bodybuilding and body-reducing supplements on the market. Look for quality when buying these products. Are the protein efficiency rations (PER) high? Do the products contain essential vitamins, minerals, amino acids, and digestive enzymes? Often the advantage of supplementation for a woman bodybuilder is that she can feed her body added nutrients *without* necessarily increasing the overall caloric content of her food intake. This is particularly useful to a woman during the important precontest period.

Also, for those wanting to add calories to their diets, weight-gain products can furnish high-quality nutrition and extra calories while lessening the burden of digestion, which could prove a problem if regular foods are taken. There is also an added convenience factor to consider. Often a nutrient-loaded milkshake is easier, and more fun, to prepare than a formal meal. The modern woman bodybuilder takes advantage of scientific supplementation, and makes it work by tailoring certain products to her specific requirements.

Steroids

What are anabolic steroids? They are artificial derivatives of the male hormone testosterone. Normal men and women have hormones from *both* sexes in their bodies. Needless to say, a man has considerably more testosterone than estrogen (the female hormone), and women have more estrogen than the male hormone.

Unfortunately, some women take anabolic steroids, which serve to make their bodies more masculine. They get stronger, more muscular, and tend to shed fat more easily, especially in the hip and leg area where many women have a tendency to store fat. Dangerous side effects for women can include increased hairiness, a deeper voice, aggressive behavior, diminishment of breasts, a premature aging of the muscle cells, among others.

Steroids were developed in Germany around 1936. They were given to sick people with muscle-wasting diseases and chronically weak post-operative patients in hospitals to help build up their weight to normal levels. Today physicians often freely prescribe these potentially dangerous drugs, not to the sick,

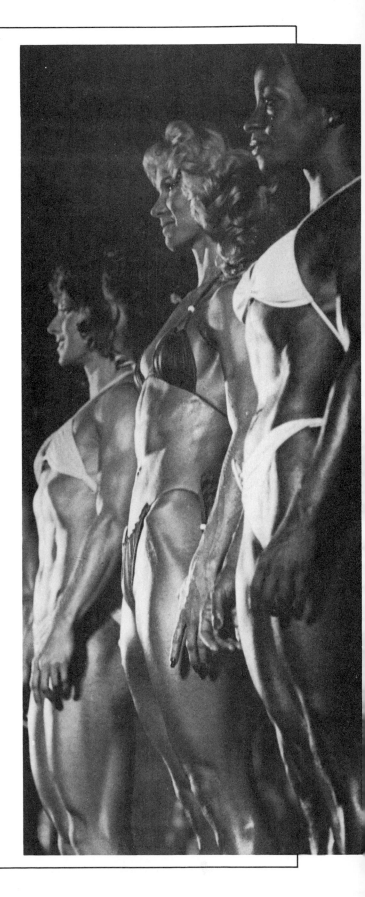

but to the healthy. They are dished out to runners, field athletes, football players, weightlifters and bodybuilders at a staggering amount totalling in the millions of dollars annually.

A woman who takes anabolic steroids is actually trying to change her body into that of a man (sex change operations are preceded by two years of hormone therapy), yet some women have an inordinate willingness to take abusive steroid drugs, with seeming disregard for the dangerous side effects.

In women's bodybuilding contests, points are awarded for the degree of proportionate muscle size and for low body-fat levels and well-defined ("ripped") muscles. These results can be obtained the healthy way—from steady, progressive training and precontest dieting, both of which are covered completely in this book. Do not jeopardize your health by playing Russian roulette with anabolic steroids.

Although steroids work on all the tissues of the body, including the hormone-sensitive receptors on the ovaries and in the pituitary and hypothalamus glands, their effect on a woman's reproductive system is not known. Indeed, if she were to have children, would they be abnormally affected?

Women were first accused of using steroids only a decade or two ago. It was initially prompted by the masculine appearance of some of the Russian Olympic athletes in track and field. By the mid-70s women were definitely linked with taking steroids—first the track and field athletes, then powerlifters, and now, in ever-increasing numbers, women bodybuilders. Very few will admit it. Although we are vehemently against the use of steroids by both sexes, a woman taking artificial male hormones is particularly unwise.

Women bodybuilders who have been in the sport a number of years tend not to resort to drug use. However, those new to bodybuilding can't wait for natural results and many try steroids almost from the beginning, because they want their bodies developed overnight.

It is estimated that almost 30 percent of women competing in top bodybuilding contests are using anabolic steroids. While we are not happy with this statistic, it should be noted that no steroid abuser has ever won the prestigious IFBB Ms. Olympia contest, generally recognized as the highest bodybuilding accolade a woman can attain.

Steroids are not illegal drugs. They are not controlled substances, but they require a prescription to legally obtain them. There is definitely an aspect of ignorance associated with women who take steroids—if they knew the potential dangers, surely they would not take them. Many women bodybuilders are wives or girlfriends of male bodybuilders. Unfortunately, there is ample evidence that often the men talk the women into taking steroids.

Some women even make the decision on their own. For example, a woman may have trained for several years only to enter a contest and be beaten by some neophyte who has only been lifting weights for eight months, but who has taken steroids. There is a justified animosity between those who would never take artificial steroids and those who do.

It is not uncommon for a woman bodybuilder using steroids to transform the muscularity and size of her body within a three-month period. Such a dramatic and *fast* change is not reasonable to expect from *natural* (non-steroid) training.

Drug tests are on the way. The IFBB has already instituted steroid tests for amateurs, and the pros are next in line. There have been problems in the past with the financing of tests, since the procedure is enormously expensive.

Women's bodybuilding as a sport suffers from this steroid connection. Even though the majority of competitors, and almost all noncompetitors, do *not* take drugs, the word is out that the more muscular women do take them. Athletic organizations are taking strong stands against them, in agreement with the IFBB. The sooner we close the chapter on steroid abuse, the better off the sport will be.

THE LEAN ADVANTAGE

Gladys Portugues

Beating the Fat Problem

This chapter is for women who weigh more than the accepted 5–8 pounds above their ideal competitive weight. If you are one of these women, then you may be up to 30, 40, or even more pounds overweight. Or perhaps you just want to shed 10–15 pounds. Whatever the case, the strategy is the same.

It would be remiss of us to repeat what so many misleading diet books have said before, that you do not need to have willpower, that

Rachel McLish and Cory Everson compare backs.

there is no need to count calories, that you will not have any hunger pangs. Losing weight takes conscious effort.

Why are you overweight right now? According to Dr. Stuart Berger, author of the Southampton diet, "The basic causes of being overweight, whether 2 or 200 pounds, are almost always psychological. There are scores of factors tracing back to a variety of emotional conflicts."

An example of this psychological situation could be characterized by your mother breast feeding or bottle feeding you as a baby when you were crying. The milk would act as compensation for your upset state of mind. Similarly, as a child you could be rewarded with a chocolate bar or a box of cookies to cheer you up after falling or hurting yourself, or being upset over a certain social situation. If you ate the chocolate or cookies, then you might have felt an immediate sense of relief and gratification. There is no doubt that oral stimulation (eating) provides quick relief for emotional distress.

As a result, we may become accustomed to using food as an oral "pacifier." It comforts us. Unfortunately, these binges also often create new fat cells. Being fat often creates its *own* emotional upset. If we see ourselves as unattractive to other people, we may withdraw from social relationships. This gives us a strong sense of emptiness and deprivation, even depression, all of which we fight off by overeating. Now we really are compounding the problem. We are trapped in a vicious circle of eating in order to ward off emotional problems; and the very act of eating brings us more unhappiness.

The key to weight reduction is diet. Never make the mistake of cutting your calorie intake in half. Drastic cuts are just *not* workable—neither is fasting. Both practices put your body in shock; you would either subject yourself to an unbearable headache, or else your hunger pangs would be severe.

However, more importantly, cutting off your food supply in a drastic manner doesn't necessarily work as well as you may imagine. Invariably the body reacts by bracing itself for the famine by storing extra fat on which to live. Many scientific studies have shown that harsh, unbalanced diets or fasts actually cause the body to become fatter. More fat-depositing enzymes are produced and create what Covert Baily, the author of *Fit or Fat*, describes as the fat person's chemistry, a *tendency to get fat*.

An overweight person's diet must be reduced in stages. Start by just dropping all sugar from the diet, then reduce all calorie-dense snacks, such as chocolate and candies, then take out cakes, cookies, and butter. Get all the junk foods out. Once you have a balanced diet of fruits, vegetables, whole cereals, poultry, lean meat, fish, milk and milk products, you can carry on the gradual reduction of overall calories consumed while still keeping a balanced food intake.

Yes, food intake is the key, but there is another side to weight reduction—*aerobic exercise*. As we stated before, aerobic exercise is any disciplined, repetitive action that induces an oxygen debt. In other words, an exercise that keeps your heart level comfortably elevated for 15–20 minutes.

Weight training is considered by some experts to be an anaerobic activity (without oxygen), although it is obvious that a person who keeps increasing the pace in their weight workouts could get an aerobic effect. Weight training burns almost no fat, because fat cannot be converted quickly enough to energy. Aerobic activities, however, are low-intensity and can (should) be continued for long periods of time. The beauty of aerobic exercise is that, unlike high-intensity effort, energy comes from the body's store of fat.

Aerobics should be practiced at least twice a week, preferably three times. As you get fitter and more enthusiastic you can increase aerobic activity to five or even six times weekly. Exercise that requires 80 percent of your maximum heart rate, or lower, is considered aerobic. If you push your heart to

Candy Csencsits

tivities because they keep your heart well below 80 percent of maximum rate.

Once you have normalized your bodyweight using aerobic exercise and a calorie-reduced diet, make sure that you do not allow yourself to develop bad habits again. Your aim should be to maintain a low percentage of body fat for the rest of your life! This, in the early stages, will probably prove to be one of the most difficult things you have ever done. Why? Because you will have to eliminate all of those bad eating habits that developed fat in the first place. If you look at it one way, you could interpret this to mean that you will have to constantly be on a diet. We prefer to think of it as a *revised* attitude towards food. We want you to establish and understand fully that what you have been eating in the past (both the quality and quantity) was unacceptable. You must now overhaul and revise your past nutritional habits. You must be put in touch with your true need for wholesome, unadulterated foods, and eat them only when you are genuinely hungry. This may sound like a tall order. All we can say is: Master it and you will be putting yourself in line for a longer, healthier, fitter, pain-free existence of self-contentment and joy.

Muscle Size

The world's greatest artists throughout history have paid homage to the beauty of the female body. From the ancient Venus de Milo in the Louvre Museum in Paris to the modern artists of today, the form of the feminine physique was represented by all those with the ability to transcribe shape to canvas or marble.

And then came women's bodybuilding.

Probably the most visible of the modern-day promoters of the sport of women's bodybuilding is Lisa Lyon. She has no doubts about the present situation. "Women's bodybuilding has taken a wrong turn," she says. "What I see now is exactly what I fought so hard to remove from the minds of bodybuilding skeptics

higher than 80 percent of its maximum (as is often the case with vigorous weight training), then the exercise is labelled anaerobic. To find out an estimate of your maximum heart rate, subtract your age from 220. Moderately paced swimming or brisk walking are aerobic ac-

some years ago. I see a bunch of men parading in women's bikinis. I am very disappointed with the new direction of feminine bodybuilding."

Laura Combes, a competitive bodybuilder with somewhat more muscle mass than Lisa Lyon, represents the other side of the controversy. "First and foremost a woman bodybuilder should have muscle mass, just as male bodybuilders do. After all, someone who looks like a swimmer or distance runner will never win a Mr. America title. If male bodybuilders need large muscles to win, then so should female bodybuilders. They should have fully developed, round muscles. Anything less makes women competitors beauty pageant contestants, *not* bodybuilders."

The next phase of women's bodybuilding saw the acceptance of muscles on women. And they came in all shapes and sizes—big muscles, stringy muscles, disproportionate muscles, and beautiful muscles. Suddenly, it was okay for women to be muscular, but there was still no conscious direction for the sport of women's bodybuilding. It seemed that the men had gone through a similar evolution. It took Frank Zane to exhibit the two most important aspects of bodybuilding—proportion and definition. Now the women were finding out for themselves:

- The muscles have to be developed in proportion to one another.

- The muscles must be relatively free from fat, which detracts from the shape and contour.

Now women with muscle size were passed over by the judges, who favored the "ripped" look (muscles sharply defined with cross striations and crevices). Some women, however, went overboard and got so ripped that there was very little muscle there to appraise, turning up at contests with nine-inch emaciated arms and legs and torso to match. Others had balanced physiques but the trained look was missing.

Julie McNew

The answer to all this, of course, is that a woman bodybuilder must develop a balanced physique for a contest. She can't come in with one dynamic body part and hope to win. Neither can a woman expect to get the judges' votes if she is cut to ribbons, yet has little else.

Carolyn Cheshire

It's not like the men. Male bodybuilders have comparable physiques. They possess wide shoulders and narrow hips (not all women have this V-shape by virtue of their skeletal frame). Men strive for balanced maximum muscle size and are able to cause muscle hypertrophy simply because they are men. Many women can't pack on the thick, dense musculature that men do.

There are exceptions, of course. Some women are capable of becoming massive, and they seem to overshadow their slighter sisters. Why penalize one or the other type when both have trained just as strenuously?

There is a wide range of different body shapes among female bodybuilders. Some women are broad-shouldered and narrow-hipped, while others have the petite, traditionally feminine build tailored with muscle without being overpowering. Consider the contrast between Pillow and Candy Csencsits. Naturally, this

range of female physiques creates a problem.

Joe Weider, who soon noticed that there were definitely *two* distinct camps for women's bodybuilding, has offered the idea for holding two different types of events.

Some women can muscle up almost as much as men. They get big and ripped at the same time. A lot of effort goes into that achievement and it should be rewarded. But some women will *never* look like that, no matter how hard they train. They just don't have the same chemistry. The second physique is more feline, slimmer. Two distinct builds—each deserves to win.

Both realize their potential in ways that result in two different body shapes. But a stocky, muscular woman can't be compared to a woman who has a refined, slender build.

In one contest we could have the two categories. This will satisfy the beef-cake-hungry crowd that's interested only in densely muscled women. This will also satisfy the general public, which sees bodybuilding as a sport in which a slight woman who trains to improve her appearance can win.

Joe Weider points out that at almost every women's contest he attends, a portion of the crowd is unhappy with the results. The muscle fanatics want to see huge women fighting it out for muscular supremacy. "After all," they exclaim, "the name of the game is *bodybuilding*. Anything less than all-out muscle size is a cop-out."

And then there are the advocates of the well-developed, symmetrical physique. To them, larger muscles on a woman is just not acceptable.

The IFBB at present is holding to just one ideal. Whereas they realize the observations made by Joe Weider as indisputable truth, perhaps they are afraid that the Beef It! brigade would bring out every abnormally balanced hormone freak in the land. Worse, those crazed enough for a win at any cost may resort to positively dangerous doses of artificial anabolic steroids.

The IFBB rules are stated clearly:

First and foremost, the judge must bear in mind that he or she is judging a women's bodybuilding competition and is looking for an ideal feminine physique. Therefore, the most important aspect is shape, feminine shape. The other aspects are similar to men, but in regard to muscular development, it must not be carried to excess where it resembles the massive muscularity of the male physique.

The above criteria should be clear enough. Huge muscles and immense "cuts" are out. Trained femininity is in. Women's bodybuilding has passed through many stages in the last few years. Now it has a concise and clear direction.

- A woman bodybuilder should have a well-built, healthy, strong-looking body.
- She should have well-set bones, perfect posture and deportment.
- The muscles should be fully toned and well-defined to show pleasing shape, balanced proportion and symmetry.
- Femininity and beauty are still a part of women's bodybuilding. Harmony, confidence, grace, and fitness are positive attributes.

Cory Everson

PERFECT PROPORTIONS

Dr. Lynn Pirie works out on the parallel bars.

Muscle Where It Counts

The essence of bodybuilding is to develop balanced proportion. This applies to men as well as women. But somehow the women seem to be able to better understand the idea than men. We have yet to meet a women bodybuilder who isn't very aware of her symmetry. When things are not in perfect harmony she is worried, and certainly a great deal of time is spent in trying to attain balance.

Women have more common sense than men about how they look. This probably is due to some deep-rooted behavioral pattern whereby prehistoric men were the aggressive hunters while the women were taking care of the home and family. Today this has translated into men wanting to build impressive muscles whereas women have a need only for aesthetic muscles.

shape, but also is famous for training many of the stars of bodybuilding, stage, and screen, explains: "Although a muscle has four sides, and each aspect has to be trained, that does not mean that you should train each part of a muscle equally hard." In other words, he is saying that in the name of *visual perfection*, we should bring out certain muscle parts more than others, to dramatize the illusion. Nothing is more absurd than trying to maximize every part of every muscle.

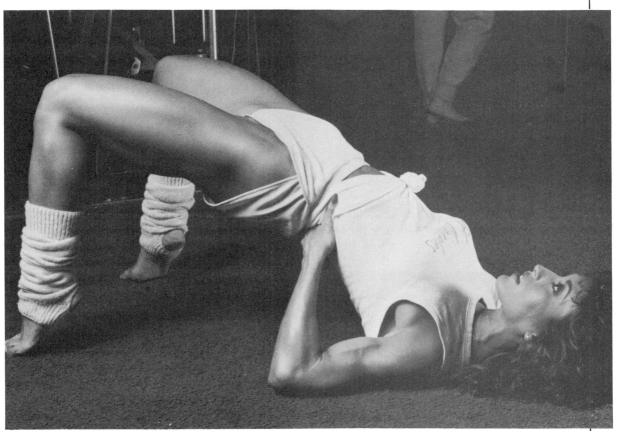

Rachel McLish stretches out before a workout.

Balanced proportion does not just occur by itself. You have to first *think* about it, then *plan* for it, and subsequently *train* for it. Like a sculptor or architect, a bodybuilder must always be aware of what she's doing. She must work for physical balance.

Vince Gironda, a man in his sixties, who has not only trained himself to prize-winning

Let's talk briefly about the various body parts, detailing how you can utilize the correct training approach to create the best results.

Most women are aware of the effect that clothes can have on their appearance. Puffy sleeves will do wonders for rounded, small shoulders. Well-cut pants can make hips look

Kay Baxter

more slender. High-heeled shoes can create an illusion of longer legs.

Just as you can use clothes to hide or accentuate certain body parts, you can tailor your muscles to highlight your overall physique. Add a bit here, take away there, and presto! Before you know it, your complete dynamic physique is emerging. Here are some tips:

Shoulders

Build the side (lateral head) if you are too narrow in this region. Dumbbell lateral raises will do the job. If your shoulders are rounded or drooping forward, then incorporate plenty of dumbbell bent-over raises and T-bar rows in your workout to work the rear head (posterior deltoid).

Lats

The lats, (short for latissimus dorsi), being the largest back muscles and those most responsible for that dramatic V-shape, should be worked hard to improve their flair. This taper is arrived at, not just by building the lats, but also by stretching out the scapula (the shoulder blades) of the upper back. Wide-grip chins and pulldowns contribute to this desired result.

If you want to develop more lower lat (careful now—too much lower lat can ruin the taper), then do plenty of T-bar rowing and seated cable pulls, always pulling the handles towards the waist area.

Calves

If you need more development of the *outside* of the calves, then do your heel raise exercises with the toes pointing *inward*. Development on the *inside* of the calf is achieved by performing your calf raises with the toes pointed *outward*.

For best overall shape of the lower leg, exercise with your bodyweight mainly on the big toe. Unfortunately, many women are limited by lack of mobility in the ankle joint. For best results, you must have as full a range of motion as possible, which means going upwards and downwards all the way.

The bottom part of the lower leg (the soleus) is exercised by utilizing the seated calf-raise machine.

Thighs

Upper thighs and hips are worked most vigorously with the squat and lunge exercises. Lower thighs are brought into play when the body leans rearwards during squatting movements, such as hack-lift exercises.

Biceps

The best exercises for developing the peak of the biceps are the 45-degree incline dumbbell curl, the preacher bench curl with the angle of the bench pad set at 90 degrees (vertical). Working the lower biceps is accomplished by setting the preacher bench at a shallow angle of about 25 degrees (almost horizontal).

Triceps

If you build up your triceps high near the deltoid (shoulder), your arm will appear to

Mary Roberts pushes out a set of incline flyes.

taper from the shoulder to a diminishing elbow region. It would be more aesthetically pleasing to have the upper-arm muscles gradually tucking neatly into the elbow region.

If you have too much triceps bulk near the shoulder, avoid the lying triceps curl. Perform the single-arm triceps extension while in the seated or standing position. Another good exercise for the lower triceps is the back press with strands and the standing close-grip barbell (or E-Z curl bar) stretch behind the head, holding the elbows as close to the ears as possible. The best lower triceps movement is the bent-over dumbbell extension to the rear (with your torso and upper arm parallel to the floor).

Abdominals

Since bodybuilding contests are increasing in popularity and money prizes, the bodybuilder is finding that she has to develop every inch of her body for success. In the old days it was quite acceptable if a contestant had only a couple of rows of abdominal muscles to show the judges; today she has to have abs above *and* below the navel.

In addition to the hanging leg raise, which is the best exercise for the lower abs described in the section on abdominals, another good exercise is the Roman chair sit-up, whereby the body is lowered below the hips in each repetition.

Chest

It is important to fully develop the outer areas of the pectoral muscles to accentuate the V-shape flair of the torso. This is done with wide-grip parallel bar dips (if you can do them) and incline and flat flye exercises with dumbbells. Wide-grip bench presses also develop this area.

When a woman sets out on a course to build and shape her body, it makes sense to only build muscle in the areas where it will look attractive and add to her overall appearance. Bodybuilding is not a haphazard

sport. It is not even a matter of "maxing out" every muscle. What you are doing is restyling your entire physique. Do it right from the start and you won't have to *undo* any of your hard work later.

Posture

Good posture is important for everyone. It is achieved when all the elements of the body are balanced vertically on each other. When we walk, run, or engage in various activities this alignment changes. For example, the upper body tends to lean or "fall" forward as we walk.

The word *posture* indicates the manner in which we carry the body when standing, sitting, or walking. You change posture every time you change your activity. This constant change becomes second nature to us. We get into the habit of either sitting correctly or lazily. It's easy to develop poor posture, and this is where the trouble begins. If you practice bad posture long enough, it will become habitual. The same is true, of course, with good posture. Practice it and it can become you.

In spite of the fact that an upright stance is a woman's natural position, most people droop and become round shouldered. To avoid this "stoop," make a constant effort to correct your posture throughout the day.

Correct posture is really the most relaxing posture. Curiously enough, those who think they are relaxing by slouching are really causing added fatigue to set in. Watch people walking or sitting just about anywhere. Many of them are slouching, which is usually an indication of physical weakness. Bad posture can contribute to illness. Lungs can be cramped; your stomach, liver, and other abdominal organs can be crowded and dislodged.

A woman who stands well—upright and proud—holds within her a beauty asset. And good posture aids verbal expression. In his book *Exercise*, Dr. Herbert M. Shelton states:

Mohamed Makkawy and Gladys Portugues

Dinah Anderson

Lordosis

The abnormal forward tilting of the pelvis. This condition contributes to general abdominal malfunctions.

Kyphosis

This results when the upper back is overly rounded. Combined, as it often is, with lordosis, it is called *kyphlordosis*.

Side Balance

Disturbed lateral balance of the spinal column gives unequal shoulder height (one is lower than the other). This can result from one leg being shorter than the other, or from a tilted pelvis, but more often than not it results from poor control habits.

It is true that sometimes postural defects are inherited, such as a shorter leg or some structural fault in the spine or pelvis, but most irregularities are caused by poor habits, such as sitting with one leg under the other (which causes abdominal deterioration and curved upper back).

There are certain postural malfunctions that are beyond immediate control, but most are preventable and remediable. Most can be corrected by postural awareness and by regular practice of correctional exercises. Here are a few specific corrective exercises for particular problems.

Drooping Head

Sit upright in a chair, with your chin touching your upper chest. Clasp hands behind head and raise your head while resisting strongly with your hands. Do one set of fifteen repetitions.

Round Shoulders

Sit with hands clasped behind your head, keeping your back and head in a straight line. With hands behind your head, spread your elbows as far back as possible, tightening the upper-back muscles to their limit. Do this exercise every day for one set of ten repetitions.

Upon the upright attitude depends the usefulness of the senses, complete respiration, the ability to talk, speak or read with correct tone of force and the most efficient use of the body. Erect carriage is exceedingly important to the health and vigor as well as the best appearance of man and woman.

There is no doubt that to secure the best results in function and appearance of your body, all of your structures must be properly aligned. Poor posture can result in stress and strain, which may cause discomfort and pain. The following postural maladies are common to many people.

Uneven Shoulders

Hold a dumbbell (about ten to twenty pounds) in the hand of the shoulder that is low. Simply shrug that shoulder, keeping the arm straight, for one set of fifteen repetitions.

Few exercises in themselves will correct poor posture. Sports or athletic pursuits will help slightly. Some sports even contribute to severe postural defects. Judo and figure skating cause lower back hollowness. Cycling can round upper backs. However, most sports strengthen the overall skeletal muscles. Weight training does it better, because *all* the muscles are involved.

Remember, postural improvement will result from overall strengthening exercises plus constant attention to correcting your stance whenever you catch yourself slouching or drooping. Severe postural problems should, of course, be referred to your doctor.

Dumbbell triceps extensions are performed by Rachel McLish.

THE WORKOUT ROUTINE

Gladys Portugues works her biceps on the preacher bench.

Putting It Together

There are many important points to consider when compiling your routine. Surely, it is more than stringing a few exercises together.

Before you put pen to paper and write out your own super routine, consider the following recommendations.

Exercise all body parts.

Even if you feel that your upper body and arms are pretty good, and that you only need to work your legs and waistline, don't do it. Every basic area must be trained. You must keep maximum tone in each area of your body. It is a big mistake to think that you only need to exercise certain body parts.

Do not make your routine too long.

It would be nice to be able to do every exercise known. But that's an impossibility. You have to work within your ability to recuperate and within the capacity of your energy levels. If your routine is too short, there is a likelihood that you are not exercising all major body parts. A routine that is too long causes overtraining, which is worse. It has a negative effect on the body and will ultimately lock you into a sticking point; in some cases it causes the body's immune system to be more susceptible to viruses and sickness.

Perform exercises with a specific goal.

Each exercise you choose should be selected to accomplish a certain goal. Don't waste your time squatting if your upper thighs are already too big and muscular. Perform hack slides instead. Forget the heavy lateral raises if your shoulders are already wide enough. Do specific peak exercises if you have no biceps height. Go for more lower abdominal work if you have little muscularity in the area. Add plenty of pulldowns and chins if your back is lacking in V-shape. You must tailor your workout exercises to your specific aims.

Do a workable workout frequency.

Is there a golden rule about workout frequency? Well, not really, but there's a well-tested guideline to follow. *A muscle should be worked two or three times a week.* That's it, right there.

If you train a specific muscle or muscle group less than twice a week, you will find that beyond a certain point you cannot continue to make progress. The frequency is not

Rachel McLish demonstrates a toe raise for the calf muscles.

Lori Bowen-Rice does a lat-machine pressdown.

enough to allow for continued results. As a start, build your workout frequency around training each body part either two or three times a week.

Believe it or not, there are hundreds of frequency variations that you can use. The most common way to train, still used by more weight trainers than any other, is three whole-body workouts a week, with at least a day's rest between each one. Quite often this translates into training Mondays, Wednesdays, and Fridays, although, of course, there are many other combinations.

Another way to arrange your training (especially if you have a long schedule) is to split it into two parts. Simply perform half your workout one day and half the next. Some trainers like to split their schedule by working upper body one workout and lower body the next workout. If you train four days a week on a split routine, you will work every body part

twice a week. If you train six days a week, you will hit each area three times a week.

You have another alternative, though, known as the *every-other-day split*. It works like this: You split your workout routine in two as previously mentioned. The first part of the routine is performed one day, then you rest completely the next day; the day after that you work the second half of the routine, and rest again the following day. And so on. This method actually gives your muscle groups two workouts one week and three workouts the next. It has been found ideal for off-season training and is especially beneficial for those with limited time. Perfect recuperation is all but guaranteed for those following this routine.

Yet another form of varying training frequency is to split your entire routine into three parts instead of two. You can train one-third on the first day, one-third on the second day, and one-third on the third day. You will of course, have to train a minimum of six days in a row to maintain the recommended twice-a-week workout for each muscle group.

Training frequency can get a little complicated. Not everyone can train just when they want to. Many gyms are not open on Sundays, and some of us have shift work, overtime, or school hours that do not always fit in easily with training requirements. You just have to do the best you can in difficult circumstances. Where there's a will there's a way.

If you experiment with different training frequencies, you will discover that you soon learn what suits your particular case and what does not. If you find yourself getting overtired, then either shorten your routine or change your workout frequency. Remember, you do not have to work within the limitations of a seven-day week. Many women enjoy working the *three-days-on, one-day-off routine*. They split their routine into *two* parts, and train for *three* days in a row (first half of routine, second half of routine, first half of routine), then they rest a day before beginning the cycle again.

The following are some suggested routines for women at all levels.

The Beginner's Routine

It is probably best for the beginner to train three times a week, with a rest day in between each workout. Do not try to use heavy weights at first. Perform your exercises in good (strict) style. Complete beginners should only perform one set of each exercise, but after a few weeks you should be able to do two or three.

Warm-up (Heart Pulse)
Rope Jumping—1½ minutes
Pectorals (Chest)
Bench Press—3 sets × 8 reps
Thighs (Upper Legs)
Squat—3 sets × 10 reps
Deltoids (Shoulders)
Dumbbell Press—3 sets × 8 reps
Lats (Upper Back)
Wide-grip Pulldown—3 sets × 10 reps
Calves (Lower Legs)
Standing Calf Raise—3 sets × 20 reps
Abdominals (Midsection)
Crunches—3 sets × 15 reps
Triceps (Back of Arms)
Lying Triceps
   Stretch—3 sets × 10 reps
Biceps (Front of Arms)
Barbell Curl—3 sets × 8 reps

The Strength-Building Routine

Strength-training routines are traditionally short because the number of exercises are limited. You work the large muscles when training for overall power. Strength training means more sets, less reps, and more rest time between heavy sets (up to four minutes).

Warm-up (Heart Pulse)
Rope Jumping—1½ minutes
Pectorals (Chest)
Bench Press—8 sets × 4–6 reps
Thighs (Upper Legs)
Squat—8 sets × 4–6 reps
Deltoids (Shoulders)
Press behind Neck—
   6 sets × 5 reps
Erectors (Lower Back)
Deadlift—6 sets × 4 reps
Lats (Upper Back)
T-bar Row—6 sets × 6 reps

The Short Routine

Obviously, you must make every effort to get a quality workout in a short period of time, but you must use caution. Each exercise has two sets. Your first set must still act as a *warm-up* set. For the second set you must give everything a maximum effort.

Pectorals (Chest)
Dumbbell Bench Press—2 sets × 12 reps
Lats (Upper Back)
Parallel-grip Bar
   Pulldown—2 sets × 12 reps
Deltoids (Shoulders)
Upright Row—2 sets × 12 reps
Thighs (Upper Legs)
Hack Lift—2 sets × 12 reps
Triceps (Back of Arms)
Close-grip Bench
   Press—2 sets × 10 reps
Biceps (Front of Arms)
Incline Dumbbell
   Curl—2 sets × 8 reps
Forearms (Lower Arms)
Wrist Curl—2 sets × 15 reps
Calves (Lower Legs)
Standing Calf Raise—2 sets × 25 reps
Abdominals (Midsection)
Roman Chair Sit-up—2 sets × 25 reps

The Basic Routine

As the name implies, this routine exercises the basic muscle groups. It is abbreviated, yet adequate as a maintenance off-season routine. Because the sets are limited, we advise you to do a high-intensity workout. Push hard at the end of the set, especially the last set of each exercise. Be sure, however, to maintain good exercise form.

Warm-up (Heart Pulse)
Rope Jumping—1½ minutes
Deltoids (Shoulders)
Press behind Neck—3 sets × 8 reps
Thighs (Upper Legs)
Squat—3 sets × 10 reps
Pectorals (Chest)
Bench Press—3 sets × 8 reps
Lats (Upper Back)
Bent-over Row—3 sets × 10 reps
Calves (Lower Legs)
Calf Raise—3 sets × 25 reps
Biceps (Front of Arms)
Barbell Curl—3 sets × 10 reps
Triceps (Back of Arms)
Triceps Stretch—3 sets × 12 reps
Abdominals (Midsection)
Crunches—3 sets × 20 reps

The Leg-Specialization Routine

"Specialization" means that you put more effort into additional exercises for a specific body area. It does *not* mean that you stop working the other body parts. You still exercise them with a moderate amount of work. Because you are trying to improve one section of your body (an underdeveloped section) more than the others, you should perform these exercises first in your routine, while you have a high-energy level and can give your best to the exercises.

Warm-up (Heart Pulse)
Rope Jumping—2 minutes
Thighs (Upper Legs)
Squat—4 sets × 8 reps
Hack Machine—3 sets × 8 reps
High Extension—4 sets × 12 reps
Thigh Curl—4 sets × 12 reps
Lunge—1 set × 12 reps
Sissy Squat—2 sets × 20 reps
Calves (Lower Leg)
Standing Calf Raise—4 sets × 20 reps
Seated Calf Raise—4 sets × 20 reps
Donkey Calf Raise—4 sets × 20 reps
Pectorals (Chest)
Bench Press—3 sets × 10 reps
Deltoids (Shoulders)
Upright Row—3 sets × 10 reps
Lats (Upper Back)
Single-arm Dumbbell Row—3 sets × 8 reps
Biceps (Front of Arms)
Barbell Curl—3 sets × 8 reps
Triceps (Back of Arms)
Triceps Pressdown—3 sets × 10 reps
Forearms (Lower Arms)
Wrist Curl—3 sets × 15 reps
Abdominals (Midsection)
Hanging Knee Raise—3 sets × 20 reps

The Chest-Specialization Routine

Because this routine specializes on the chest, all the pectoral exercises are grouped at the beginning of the workout. Note that we start off with the heavier chest exercises first, finishing with the pec-isolation movements.

Warm-up (Heart Pulse)
Rope Jumping—2 minutes
Pectorals (Chest)
Bench Press—5 sets × 8 reps
Incline Bench Press—4 sets × 8 reps
Parallel Bar Dip—3 sets × 8 reps
Cross-bench Dumbbell Pullover—
    3 sets × 12 reps

Dumbbell Flye—3 sets × 12 reps
Pec-Deck Flye—2 sets × 12 reps

Thighs (Upper Legs)
Hack Lift—3 sets × 10 reps
Thigh Curl—3 sets × 12 reps

Deltoids (Shoulders)
Upright Row—3 sets × 10 reps

Lats (Upper Back)
Close-grip Pulldown—3 sets × 12 reps

Triceps (Back of Arms)
Triceps Pressdown—3 sets × 12 reps

Biceps (Front of Arms)
Preacher Bench
   Barbell Curl—3 sets × 10 reps

Forearms (Lower Arms)
Behind-back Wrist Curl—3 sets × 15 reps

Calves (Lower Legs)
Seated Calf Raise—3 sets × 20 reps

Erectors (Lower Back)
Good-morning Exercise—2 sets × 15 reps

Abdominals (Midsection)
Bench Crunches—3 sets × 12 reps

The Back-Specialization Routine

The back needs to be exercised from different angles because of the many different muscles involved—the rhomboids, latissimus dorsi, trapezius, and erector spinae. As with all specialization programs, begin your routine with the emphasized area.

Warm-up (Heart Pulse)
Rope Jumping—2 minutes

Back (Overall)
Wide-grip Chin—4 sets × 10 reps
T-bar Row—4 sets × 8 reps
Wide-grip Pulldown—3 sets × 12 reps
Narrow-grip Pulldown—3 sets × 12 reps
Incline Dumbbell Row—2 sets × 10 reps
Prone Hyperextension—2 sets × 15 reps

Pectorals (Chest)
Incline Bench Press—3 sets × 10 reps

Linda Assam performs a T-bar row for her lower-back muscles.

Deltoids (Shoulders)
Seated Press behind Neck—3 sets × 8 reps

Thighs (Upper Legs)
Squat—3 sets × 8 reps
Thigh Curl—3 sets × 12 reps

Calves (Lower Legs)
Donkey Calf Raise—3 sets × 20 reps

Triceps (Back of Arms)
Standing Triceps Stretch—3 sets × 12 reps

Biceps (Front of Arms)
Alternate Dumbbell Curl—3 sets × 8 reps

Abdominals (Midsection)
Partial Sit-ups—3 sets × 15–20 reps

The Muscle-Isolation Routine

It is possible to almost isolate your muscles by using specific exercises. This type of workout results in increased separation between individual muscles. They show up more as individual units. Use lighter weights and provide direct stress to a single muscle group or segment of a group.

Warm-up (Heart Pulse)
Rope Jumping—2 minutes

Pectorals (Chest)
Dumbbell Flye—4 sets × 10 reps
Pec-Deck Flye—3 sets × 12 reps

Lats (Upper Back)
Single-arm Row—6 sets × 10 reps

Erectors (Lower Back)
Prone Hyperextension—
    3 sets × 15 reps

Deltoids (Shoulders)
Lateral Raise
    (Side Shoulders)—
    4 sets × 10 reps
Incline Face-down Flye (Rear Shoulders)—
    4 sets × 12 reps

Triceps (Back of Arms)
Single-arm Lying Triceps Stretch
    (Outer Head)—3 sets × 12 reps
Standing Triceps Stretch (Lower Triceps)—
    3 sets × 12 reps
Lying Triceps Stretch
    (Upper Triceps Belly)—
    3 sets × 10 reps

Biceps (Front of Arms)
Preacher Bench Curl—4 sets × 10 reps
Single-arm Pulley Curl—
    4 sets × 12 reps

Forearms (Lower Arms)
Wrist Curl—3 sets × 15 reps
Reverse Wrist Curl—3 sets × 15 reps

Thighs (Upper Legs)
Leg Extension—6 sets × 10 reps
Thigh Curl—4 sets × 12 reps

Calves (Lower Legs)
Standing Calf Raise—5 sets × 20 reps
Seated Calf Raise
    (Soleus)—5 sets × 20 reps

Abdominals (Midsection)
Crunches—4 sets × 15 reps
Side Bend—4 sets × 50 reps

Lat-machine pulldowns emphasize Kay Baxter's V-shaped back.

The Heavy and Light Routine

There are benefits from training both heavy and light. You maximize muscle tone, separation, and build both muscle fibre and capillary size. Additional fibre size and strength result from using the heavier weights; tone, endurance, and pump size come from the lighter work.

Warm-up (Heart Pulse)
Rope Jumping—2 minutes

Pectorals (Chest)
Bench Press—5 sets × 5 reps
Incline Dumbbell Flye—4 sets ×
    12 reps

Thighs (Upper Legs)
Squat—5 sets × 5 reps
Thigh Extension—4 sets × 12 reps
Thigh Curl—3 sets × 12 reps

Lats (Upper Back)
T-bar Row—5 sets × 5 reps
Parallel grip Bar
    Pulldown—4 sets × 12 reps

Deltoids (Shoulders)
Press behind Neck—5 sets × 6 reps
Lateral Raise—4 sets × 12 reps

Triceps (Back of Arms)
Parallel-bar dip
    (with additional weight)—5 sets ×
    5 reps
Triceps Pressdown—4 sets ×
    15 reps

Biceps (Front of Arms)
Barbell Curl—4 sets × 6 reps
Pulley Curl—4 sets × 15 reps

Calves (Lower Legs)
Standing Calf Raise—5 sets × 12 reps
Donkey Calf Raise—4 sets × 20·reps

Abdominals (Midsection)
Roman Chair Sit-up (with weight)—3 sets
    × 10 reps
Seated Bent-knee Raise—
    3 sets × 30 reps

Rest at last!
The pleasure belongs to Lori Bowen-Rice.

The Recovery Factor

After vigorous weight-training exercise, the muscle cells must have rest time and nourishment to afford the fullest possible recuperation. If you continually rework your muscles *before* they have properly recovered from the previous workout, then you will never make any noticeable gains.

One observation about recuperation is that the body is constantly learning how to do it better. The longer you train the better you become. For the best results, train your body *hard* and *long* enough so that you will recover completely by your next workout. How do you feel the morning after a workout? Alive and ready to rise to any demanding challenge, or tired and physically drained?

An exhausted "morning after" feeling is not always accompanied by sore or aching muscles. Sore muscles usually indicate that the body is recuperating, and that the healing process is underway. Actually, if there is soreness present, the muscle has *not* fully recuperated, but at least the healing process is taking place. The general opinion is that a slight degree of soreness in the muscle is ideal. It is an indication that your workout has affected the body. If the soreness is extreme, then you have overdone it, and recuperation time will take longer.

There is a fine line between stimulating your muscles into growth with more sets, or more intensity, by switching to new exercises or combinations of exercises, and overtraining whereby your muscles don't have the time to recuperate.

How can we speed up recuperation? Read the following advice.

Leg curls stress the hamstring muscles as illustrated by Lori Bowen-Rice.

Debbie Duncanson does incline bench presses to the limit.

Relaxation

The number-one answer is, of course, relaxation. When you rest, the body is in an ideal state to mend itself quickly. You should seek out the best ways to relax between your workouts. Try to put your legs up at least once a day, and read a book, or watch television. There are numerous hobbies that can help you to relax. Do whatever appeals to you most. Of course, you don't actually have to do anything. If it appeals to you, why not put your feet up and take a nap?

Stress is *not* beneficial to the body's recuperation system. It drains you, and in extreme cases can shut off adrenal gland production. If you've ever experienced severe stress or strain, you do not need to be told how debilitating it can be. When there is a threat to our existence or well-being, our digestive system shuts down, the heart and breathing rhythms falter, and adrenaline and other hormones surge throughout the body. Momentarily we are at a peak for some type of physical action (flight or fight), but ultimately we become deflated and exhausted. If this happens regularly, then your training progress will simply not amount to much.

Fresh air and sunshine do contribute to your body's recuperative ability. We hear so much about the sun causing skin cancer, but there would not be one speck of life on earth if it weren't for the sun. A prolonged lack of sunlight can cause rickets and contribute to other physical disorders. In moderation, fresh air and sunshine will help your recuperation 100 percent. Spend a few minutes, two or three times a day, breathing deeply in the great outdoors. You will energize your entire physique.

Lori Bowen-Rice knows that fresh air and sunlight help recuperation.

Dr. Lynn Pirie

Nutrition

There is a definite place for good nutrition in building and repairing the body. If you push your muscles to the limit, then you can't expect to recuperate unless they are fed correctly. The bottom line is to have at least the RDA of protein, vitamins, and minerals. If recuperation really is a problem, then we suggest you take a *Vitamin Good Life Mega Pak*, which you can buy at vitamin stores or pharmacies. You might also benefit from taking additional vitamin B complex, vitamins C and E, and some type of chelated mineral supplement.

You may discover that your recuperation is poor while you are trying to slim down or prepare for a bodybuilding contest. The reason for this is that you have probably reduced your complex carbohydrates to a level too low for muscle recuperation. Take in more vegetables and whole grains to beat the problem before it beats you. The days of precontest starvation are over.

At the very least, your diet should be able to satisfy the immediate muscle-mending requirements of your body. It was Joe Weider who said: "When recuperative functions are ailing, you better correct the causes quickly or throw in the towel."

CHEST

Rachel McLish does incline flyes for her chest muscles.

Developing the Pectorals

Women are generally enthusiastic about developing the muscles in their chest. Some advanced trainers even go so far as to perform 20–30 sets of exercises for this body part. In reality, this is far too heavy a workload and would lead to a severe case of overtraining in all but the most seasoned bodybuilders.

The granddaddy of all exercises for the chest area is the most favored and famous movement of them all—the bench press! This super exercise is also extremely versatile. You have two choices of variables:

1. You can alter the width of your hand spacing (a shoulder-width grip works the inner pecs, a wide grip works the outer pecs).

2. You can vary the position at which you lower the bar to the chest. (Lower it to the sternum or breastbone for the lower chest. Or lower it to the neck or collarbone area for the upper chest.) If you choose to lower the weight to an area of the chest between the two extreme points, then the area at which the bar touches the chest is the part that is exercised most.

The bench press is indeed a multi-faceted movement, the beauty of which is its extreme comfort of performance. You lie on your back, face up, and nothing moves but your arms. You feel very stable and relaxed while you are doing it. At first, you may find some difficulty in balancing the bar, but after a while you find the groove, and you do not have to consciously think about the mechanics of the movement.

It should be mentioned here and now that the breasts cannot be enlarged by exercise. Breasts are actually fatty tissue and cannot be developed by progressive-resistance movements (weight training). If you want larger breasts, this will come about from overall weight (fat) increase, taking birth control pills, or from silicone implants, none of which we recommend. Weight training builds the underlying muscles of the chest and it can help lift the breasts but not increase their size.

Although the bench press should form the basis of your chest workout, you probably should include at least one other exercise for the chest area. Dumbbell flyes and presses give a good stretch. Pullovers work the middle and upper chest as well as expand the rib cage. Incidentally, you cannot *significantly* enlarge the rib cage by any form of exercise. If you are born with a shallow rib cage, then no amount of stretching, deep breathing, squats, or pullovers will change it.

Gladys Portugues

By the same token, a deep barrel chest cannot be made smaller. It is true that the ribs (and other bones) do grow to accommodate additional weight and reduce when the bodyweight is lost, but these changes are minimal. The human skeleton, after normal growth has ended, does not have a huge capacity for change.

If you admire the well-defined look that top women bodybuilders get in their upper chests, do plenty of isolation moves in your chest routine. Exercises such as strict incline flying and pec-deck flyes (push the forearms together at the conclusion of each rep!) will do the trick. "Remember, though," says Dr. Lynne Pirie, "maximum striations only come at a time when you have really peaked your body for a contest or photo session, by restricing your calorie intake."

When sculpting your chest, bear in mind that all incline exercises work the upper chest, decline (head lower than body) exercises train the lower pectorals. Parallel bar dips also work the lower chest muscles, but if the dip bars are set farther apart, say 22–30 inches (55–75 cm), depending on your height (the taller you are the wider apart the bars should be), then you will strongly activate the important outer pectorals.

As with other exercises, bouncing, twisting, or lifting the hips from the bench in order to get the weight up is *not* the best way to build great pecs. On the contrary, you should use the weight correctly as a tool to achieve your goal. Here is Carolyn Cheshire's opinion on this subject: "The trick to bodybuilding is to put an overload on your muscles. The secret is not so much to get the weight up as it is to push up a heavy weight with the *isolated* strength of the muscles you are training."

Always remember to stretch the pectorals fully. After your first warm-up sets, you can really bring out the arms and fully extend the motion of the exercise. In most cases, the use of dumbbells permits more of a stretch than the use of a barbell.

Note the definition in Carolyn Cheshire's chest muscles.

Gladys Portugues is spotted by Mohamed Makkawy as she performs an incline bench press.

Bench Press
Overall Pectoral Area
(6–12 reps each set)

The standard way of performing the bench press is to lie face up on a bench. Take a grip, with your thumbs under the bar and about 2 feet (60 cm) apart, which allows the forearms to be vertical when the upper arms are parallel to the floor.

Lower the weight from the straight-arm position to the pectorals. Touch the bar lightly on the chest (no bouncing) and press upwards. Keep your elbows under the bar, and don't allow them to come close to the body.

Beginners may find that the bar starts to fall either forward or backwards, or that the weight rises unevenly because one arm is stronger than the other. Time and practice will cure these minor faults.

When you lower the bar to your chest, don't allow it to drop! Always control its descent deliberately, especially if it is a heavy weight.

Incline Bench Press
Upper Chest
(8–12 reps each set)

Start by lying on an incline bench set at a 35–40-degree angle. (More than 40 degrees will put too much emphasis on the front deltoids.) Press the barbell straight upwards, lock the elbows, and immediately lower the weight to the starting position. Keep the up-down movement going without pause. Your head should be facing upwards throughout the exercise. Keep your feet flat on the ground and do not arch the body as you press the weight upwards.

Supine Flye
Outer Pectorals
(10–12 reps each set)

Years ago this exercise was done very rigidly with light weights on the floor. Very light dumbbells were used, since the experts of the day insisted that the arms be fixed in an elbows-locked, straight position.

Kay Baxter works out with supine flyes.

Today we still insist on a fixed position, but one in which the arms are bent as though they were in a plaster cast. This takes the strain off the elbow joint, allows more weight to be used, gives you greater control and . . . yes, bigger, better-toned chest muscles!

While lying face up on a bench, with your feet planted firmly on the ground, lower and raise the dumbbells out to the side. Really go for the stretch once your muscles are warm.

Parallel Bar Dip
**Lower and Outer Pectorals
(8–20 reps each set)**

This is a wonderful chest movement, especially if the bars are set fairly wide apart—22–30 inches (55–75 cm). Narrow-set parallel bars will promote more triceps (upper arm) activity, but will still work the lower and outer pectorals. Wide-set parallel bars will benefit the upper-outer part of the chest. The visual impact of this development will make you look wide in the upper torso and shoulders.

When working the chest on the dip bars, place your thighs in front of your body, keep you head down (chin on chest), and elbows well out to the sides. Lower yourself as far downwards as possible and lock the elbows as you straighten up.

Gladys Portugues demonstrates low cable flyes.

Carla Temple demonstrates cable crossovers.

Incline Flye
**Upper and Outer Chest
(8–12 reps each set)**

Adopt a secure position on an incline bench (a 30–40-degree angle is best). Hold up a pair of light dumbbells, then allow your arms to lower slowly out to the sides. Keep elbows slightly bent throughout the exercise. Raise and lower slowly, keeping the weights under control as each repetition stretches the chest. Your feet should be firmly planted on the ground. Try and resist the temptation to arch the back.

Flat Dumbbell Bench Press
**Overall Chest
(8–10 reps each set)**

Lie on your back on a flat bench, face up, feet firmly on the floor. Take one dumbbell in either hand and starting at the chest level, palms facing forward, press the dumbbells simultaneously to the straight-arm position above the chest.

Cross-Bench Dumbbell Pullover
Upper and Middle Pectorals
(10–15 reps each set)

Lie across a flat exercise bench, holding a single dumbbell with both hands (thumbs around the bar, fingers touching the inside plate).

Keeping your arms slightly bent, raise the weight from behind the head to above the chest and back down again. This exercise helps to mobilize the rib cage. Do not begin this exercise with too heavy a weight.

Pec-Deck Flye
Overall Chest
(10–15 reps each set)

A pec-deck is a large apparatus found in most gyms, the function of which is to almost exclusively work the pectoral muscles (although some people adapt the apparatus to work the rear deltoids by sitting in the opposite position).

Hold the "grippers" as indicated and cross arms over chest by contracting the pectorals. Return to the starting position.

The cross-bench dumbbell pullover is illustrated by Rachel McLish.

THIGHS AND CALVES

The leg curl is performed by Julie McNew.

Ultrashaping the Legs

There's no doubt that leg exercises, especially squats, are very hard work. In fact, it is a well-known fact that thousands of women refuse to do any leg training at all.

Of course, all serious bodybuilders know that if they are to succeed, leg-training workouts must be executed with regularity. Women especially need leg work. It's no secret that men tend to have more fat on their legs than men, just as it's true that men accumulate more fat around their waists than women.

The major leg exercise is the squat. It simply works the thighs in a more direct and intense fashion than any other exercise. It could be argued that the leg press is actually an upside-down squat, yet without the discomfort associated with the deep-knee-bend movement. Well, it is a useful adjunct to the squat, but it loses out if a direct comparison is made.

The back squat is definitely the *growth* exercise. Fully contoured upper legs cannot be built without squatting. If you are looking for more thigh size, then you must base your workout around the regular back squat. The other upper-leg exercises, though important, are more of a supplemental nature.

Squatting is a very natural exercise, but it was not extensively used by weight trainers until the introduction of squat stands. Prior to that, lifters would first shoulder the weight after standing the barbell on end, and then they shuffled it into position across the back of their neck. It was all very time-consuming and could easily hurt the back. Thank heaven for squat stands!

In addition to squats, unless you are a beginner, you should select at least two other frontal-thigh movements and a leg-curl exercise. The hack squat works the outer thigh sweep and the lower part of the thighs near the knees. It has a certain elongating, or thigh lengthening, effect.

The popular thigh-extension exercise will not give you much development, but it has its use in that the quadriceps muscles are somewhat isolated and separated during the exercise. This, especially in conjunction with a low-calorie nutrition program, will contribute to a sleeker thigh appearance. Actually, if you lean back during this exercise to the supine position, you will notice that the muscles of the upper thigh, which run into the groin area, are also subjected to this muscle-isolating effect.

For those women who feel they have enough thigh mass, it is probably wise to do *only* shaping exercises. In such a case, you

Kike Elomaa demonstrates an alternate leg extension.

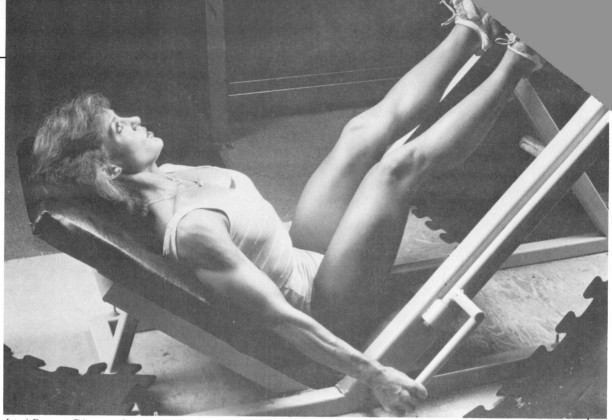

Lori Bowen-Rice works out on the leg-press machine.

may find it advantageous to use a Smith machine when performing deep-knee bends. A Smith machine, sometimes known as a press machine, has a horizontal bar that is fixed so that it can only travel upwards or downwards. Using this type of apparatus, you can squat with your feet forward of the bar, or behind it if you wish. This would be impossible if you were using a free-weight barbell from squat racks. You would fall over.

The advantage of Smith machine squats is that you can alter your foot placement to put stress on different parts of the body. For 90 percent of the training public, this stress should be on the middle and lower areas of the thigh. When using a Smith machine, the farther *forward* your feet are placed the *lower* down the leg the effect is felt. The regular back squat will build the upper thigh and glutes. Your job is to decide which is best for you, and keep to the selected style until results become evident.

The thigh biceps muscle at the back of the upper leg is an extremely important muscle to develop. If you do not build up this area,

the back of the leg will appear flat and lifeless. It will have an unaesthetic visual impact.

Thigh curls are used to work this area, and with a little ingenuity you can change the stress point to hit different parts of the thigh biceps. For example, if the apparatus were tilted to a 20–30-degree angle (head higher than legs), you would vigorously work the lower part of the biceps. By the same token, a steeper angle (some leg-press machines even allow for the exerciser to stand upright) will work the peak or highest part of the thigh biceps.

The usual method is to perform your thigh curls on a flat bench, which is a good all-around movement for hitting the belly of the area. Rachel McLish has a unique way of involving her glutes when curling her thighs. She tries to raise her thighs and hips from the padded surface of the machine at the conclusion of the leg-curl movement. Rachel also arches her back as much as possible to maximize the effect. Needless to say, less weight is used in this type of variation than would be used in the regular movement.

Thigh Exercises

Squat
Entire Thigh Area
(8–20 reps each set)

Take a barbell from a pair of squat racks and hold it at the back of your neck. You may roll a towel around the bar for added comfort. If needed, place your heels on a two-by-four-inch block of wood to improve balance. Some people just cannot squat flat-footed. It forces them to adopt a very wide stance, and even so, they are forced to lean too far forward when squatting down. Breathe in deeply before squatting. Keep your back flat and your head up throughout the movement. Breathe out forcefully as you raise upwards.

Sissy Squat
Lower Thigh and
General Sweep
(12–15 reps each set)

This is a very specialized movement designed to work the lower-thigh area. Because of the unusual angle at which the exercise is performed, this movement is done with either no weight or only a moderate poundage. (Weight can be added either by holding a barbell in front of the shoulders or by holding dumbbells at arm's length, hanging at the sides.) The name "sissy squat" is not intended to denote that the exercise is easy.

The exercise is a little tricky. Adopt a position with your feet about 12 inches (30 cm) apart. Rise upwards on your toes, and lower into a squat while leaning as far back as possible. The point to bear in mind is to keep your thigh and torso in the same plane throughout the exercise. If this is difficult, then hold the back of a chair for balance.

Dinah Anderson performs the back squat.

Candy Csencsits illustrates the lunge exercise.

Lunge
Thighs, Hips, Buttocks
(10–20 reps each set)

Place a light barbell across your shoulders. Set your feet and legs comfortably apart. From this starting position, step forward 2–3 feet (60–90 cm) with your right leg (the longer the lunge the more it involves and firms the buttocks; the shorter the movement the more the thighs are stressed), keeping your left leg slightly bent. When your right foot touches the floor, bend that leg as fully as possible. In the lunge position, your left knee should be 6–10 inches (15–25 cm) from the floor; your torso will be arched and leaning slightly forward. Return to original starting position and repeat the action with the left leg. Alternate the exercise until the prescribed number of reps have been completed.

Thigh Extension
Lower and Middle Thigh
(10–15 reps each set)

Sit on a thigh-extension machine with the tops of your feet (at the ankle flexion point) secured under the lift pad. Start raising the weight by extending both legs together. Do not kick the weight up—start the lift slowly. If the machine you are using starts to move, you are exerting too much force. Slow down and make the muscles feel it.

The thigh extension—Rachel McLish shows how.

Leg Curl
Thigh Biceps
(12–15 reps each set)

Lie on a thigh-curl machine, face down. Hook your heels under the lift bar and proceed to curl your legs upwards in unison. Concentrate on feeling the tension in the back of your legs. Do not bounce the weight up after the legs straighten; Pause and start the curl slowly and deliberately. You can prop your torso up on your elbows and raise your thighs to stress different areas.

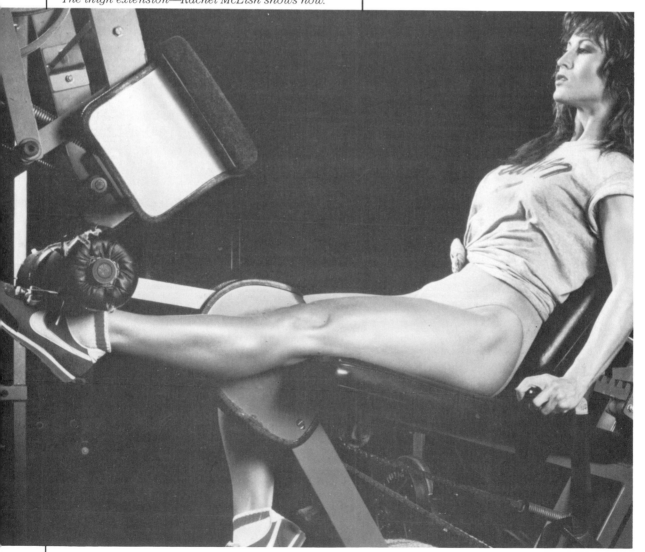

Machines are super effective for exercising the legs.

Hack Squat
**Middle and Lower Thigh
(10–15 reps each set)**

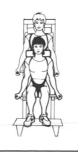

Position yourself on a hack machine. Lower and raise yourself by bending and straightening your legs. Depending on the setup of the machine, you may find it ad- vantageous to perform the exercise with your feet placed in various positions. (Heels together with toes pointing outward will de- velop the lateral section of the thigh.) Also, you may want to experiment by keeping your knees together; alternatively, you may want to hold them out to the sides.

The rear leg raise is performed by Rachel McLish.

Hack Lift
**Middle and Lower Thigh
(10–15 reps each set)**

Hold a loaded barbell be-
hind your body while standing up straight. Keep your
head up and squat down,
keeping the bar close to the
back of the legs as you do
so. Raise upwards and repeat. A two-by-four-
inch block of wood can be placed under the
heels to help balance control.

The 45-degree leg press by Lori Bowen-Rice.

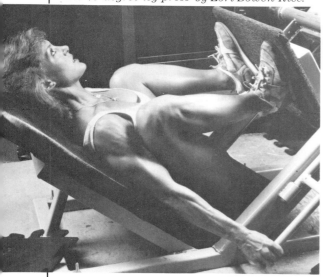

Rachel McLish presses out a toe raise.

Calf Exercises

When it comes to calf exercises the important fact is that the up-down heel movement is complete. You must strive for utmost stretch in both directions.

You will notice that the amount of repetitions recommended in lower-leg work is higher than for most other body parts. It is true that some bodybuilders seem to thrive on low or medium reps (6–10) when training this area, but the majority get better results from high reps.

Seated Calf Raise
Soleus
(15–20 reps each set)

This exercise is performed on a special leverage machine. The muscle worked in this movement is the one below the calf muscle. Perform as many heel raises as you can, concentrating on maximizing total calf stretch with each repetition. Make sure there is adequate padding on the T-hoist to fully protect the knees.

Gladys Portugues does seated calf work with her trainer Ken Wheeler.

Standing Calf Raise
Entire Calf
(15–25 reps each set)

It is important that the calf machine you use is capable of handling heavy weights. The apparatus should either carry a huge stack of weights or else be set up with a leverage benefit, so that comparatively small weights can add up to a large overall load.

Rise upwards and downwards on your toes with your legs straight and without bouncing at the bottom of the movement. Go for maximum stretch both in the up and down parts of the movement.

Single-Leg Calf Raise
Entire Calf
(15–25 reps each set)

This exercise is very similar to the standing calf raise. You may find difficulty at first if you haven't performed this one-legged variation before, but with practice you will soon get used to it. For added resistance, you may perform this exercise on a calf machine, or you may hold a heavy dumbbell in one hand while you raise upwards and downwards.

Donkey Calf Raise
Entire Gastrocnemius
(15–25 reps each set)

There is no doubt that the bent-over position you adopt for donkey calf raises does something very special for the lower legs. This exercise is a great favorite of Ms. Olympia Rachel McLish. Lean on a bench or table top so that your upper body is comfortably supported parallel to the floor. Have a training partner sit on your lower back,

Debbie Duncanson demonstrates the standing calf raise.

over the hip area. Rise upwards and downwards on your toes until you cannot perform another rep. Use a four-inch block under your toes to give greater range to the foot movement.

BICEPS AND TRICEPS

Julie McNew

Enlarging Your Arms

Women today want to develop nicely muscled, balanced arms in the same way they strive for firm-looking legs and hips.

The complete arm is made up of the forearm muscles (there are more of those than you would want to know about) and the triceps, brachialis, and biceps of the upper arm.

Actually, the forearms are brought into action in every exercise you do. Whenever you pick up a barbell or dumbbell the forearm is activated. Even when doing exercises like thigh extensions you tend to grab the side of a bench, flexing the muscles of your forearms. It's the same when squatting, deadlifting, or curling. The forearms invariably come into play. When we train the forearms with direct exercises they need many repetitions to fully stimulate them. Like the calves, they are high-rep muscles.

The biceps are, as the name suggests, a two-headed muscle. When someone says: "Show us your muscle!" they are invariably referring to the biceps. The biceps appear to be one long muscle on top of the arm that forms a bump or peak when we bend our arm and flex hard. The outer head of the biceps is exercised most when we perform close-grip curls or chins; the inside head is activated when we use a wide grip.

The preacher bench is a useful apparatus because you can vary the angle of the padded tabletop. Adjust it to an upright 90-degree angle and your curls will reward you with a high peak. Place the bench top at a shallow 35-degree angle and the stress will be placed on the lower biceps area. Perform this movement religiously and you will develop that biceps length.

The triceps have three distinct areas (heads) which act to straighten the arms. Just as you should aim to build "low" biceps, it is also a good idea to try and build "low" triceps. Nothing looks worse than high-knotted arm muscles crowding the shoulders, with no development near the elbow joint.

In our opinion, the most attractive triceps section is the outer head. This beautiful muscle is located just beneath the lateral deltoid (side shoulder) area. It is isolated in most triceps exercises where the elbows are held considerably wider than the hands.

The brachialis is not a particularly noticeable muscle in the upper arm, but its development is important if arm thickness is required. The brachialis develops from chinning and rowing exercises as much as it does from the various curling exercises.

Julie McNew works out with triceps dips.

Triceps Exercises

Lat-Machine Pressdown
Lower Triceps
(8–15 reps each set)

Start by holding a lat-machine bar with your hands 2–8 inches (5–20 cm) apart. Now press downwards until the arms are straight. Return and repeat.

Most bodybuilders keep their elbows at their sides during this movement. A few deliberately hold the elbows out to the sides and lean into the exercise. This activates the outer triceps head.

Standing Triceps Stretch
Lower Triceps
(8–12 reps each set)

Hold the weight as illustrated behind the head. Keep your elbows pointing skyward as much as possible as you perform the exercise. Raise and lower the weight rhythmically without bouncing it at the bottom of the exercise, which could strain the tendons near the elbow.

Single-arm Lying Triceps Stretch
Outside Triceps Head
(12–15 reps each set)

Lie on your back on a flat exercise bench, with your feet firmly on the floor. Hold a light dumbbell in your right hand at arm's length above your chest. Keeping the upper arm as vertical as possible, bend your elbow to lower the dumbbell to touch your left shoulder. Raise steadily and repeat. Positively *do not* bounce the weight in this exercise. Perform the same movement with the left arm.

Prone Pulley Triceps Extension
Lower and Outer Triceps
(10–15 reps each set)

Kneel on the floor holding a pulley cable with both hands. Rest your elbows on a low bench. Slowly straighten the arms against the resistance. Return under control and repeat with a steady rhythm.

Triceps extensions are demonstrated by Deborah Diana.

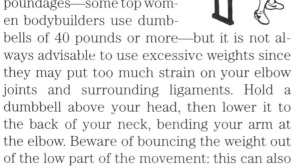

The close-grip bench press for the triceps is performed by Carla Dunlap.

Close-grip Bench Press
Lateral Triceps Head
(6–10 reps each set)

This is a great favorite with women who want to develop size quickly. Lie face up on a flat bench, feet firmly planted on the floor, holding a fairly heavy barbell (E-Z curl bars are the most popular among the pros) or have a partner hand it to you. Use a narrow grip so your hands are only 2–3 inches (5–8 cm) apart. Keeping your elbows close to your body, lower the weight to your breastbone, and immediately push upwards. You should start by using only light weights, but many women quickly work up to using over 80 pounds in this exercise.

Lying Triceps Stretch
Entire Triceps
(8–12 reps each set)

Lie on your back as shown, and hold two dumbbells at arm's length. Lower them slowly to your ears, and raise again to the starting position. This exercise works the entire triceps area. Do not use heavy weights in this exercise if you are prone to elbow soreness.

Single-arm Dumbbell Raise
Lower Triceps
(10–15 reps each set)

This triceps exercise develops the lower triceps area. With practice it is possible to handle very heavy poundages—some top women bodybuilders use dumbbells of 40 pounds or more—but it is not always advisable to use excessive weights since they may put too much strain on your elbow joints and surrounding ligaments. Hold a dumbbell above your head, then lower it to the back of your neck, bending your arm at the elbow. Beware of bouncing the weight out of the low part of the movement: this can also cause elbow problems. Make an effort to hold the upper arm close to your head during the performance of this exercise.

Reverse Triceps Dip
Triceps Belly
(10–20 reps each set)

Many women like to taper off their triceps workout with this movement. Set yourself up as illustrated using benches or chairs and dip down as low as you can each repetition. Press up immediately until your arms are straight. If you are feeling strong, you may choose to place a weight disc on your upper thighs for added resistance.

Biceps Exercises

Barbell Curl
Biceps Belly
(6–12 reps each set)

The regular barbell curl has contributed to more big arms than any other exercise. Hold the bar slightly wider than shoulder width, and keep your elbows close to your body as you curl the weight upwards until it is under your chin.

There are two distinct styles of doing this exercise: (1) strictly (no leaning backwards during the movement, starting from a straight-arm position with absolutely no body motion or "swing"), and (2) cheating (hoisting the weight up by turning the trunk of your body into a pendulum as you swing the barbell). Both methods are workable, and most successful bodybuilders get best results by doing at least the first 6–8 reps in strict style and then finishing off the harder last 3–4 reps with a cheating motion.

Incline Dumbbell Curl
Overall Biceps
(8–12 reps each set)

Lie back on an incline bench slanted at about 45 degrees. Hold two dumbbells in the arms-down position. It does not matter whether you start the movement with your palms facing towards the body or upwards. The only difference is that the forearms are brought more into play when the palms are facing the body. Curl both dumbbells simultaneously. Your seat should not come up from the bench at any time during the curl, since that would aid the biceps in getting the weight up and therefore relieve them of some of their work.

As soon as the dumbbells reach shoulder level, lower the weight and repeat. Some bodybuilders actually tense their at the end of the curl when the dumbbells shoulder level. This is just another way of maximizing the intensity of the exercise.

Seated Dumbbell Curl
Overall Biceps
(8–12 reps each set)

Sit at the end of a flat bench, holding two dumbbells. Curl both simultaneously to the shoulders and lower slowly. Try not to lean backwards as the dumbbells are curled upwards. You may perform this movement with your palms facing upwards or towards the body.

Pulley Curl
Biceps Peak
(10–15 reps each set)

Hold a pulley cable handle (attached to a low pulley) with an undergrip. Keeping the elbows close to the body, smoothly curl up the bar. If you are not used to curling with a cable attachment, you may have difficulty controlling the bar at first, but in time you will master the technique.

Alternate Dumbbell Curl
Biceps Belly
(6–10 reps each set)

This exercise is a great favorite of many champion bodybuilders. It works the biceps more directly than the two-handed dumbbell curl, since it tends to prevent cheating.

Perform the movement by standing erect and first curling one dumbbell. Then, as you lower it, curl the other arm. Lower slowly, and do not swing the bells up with any added body motion.

Rachel McLish shows her well-defined arms in an alternate dumbbell curl.

Single-arm Pulley Curl
Biceps Peak
(10–15 reps each set)
Using the low pulley cable with the single-arm attachment, place the elbow firmly at your side (or anchor it in the groin area). Start with the arms in a straight (extended) position and curl with a smooth, rhythmic action.

Inger Zetterqvist peaks her biceps on the preacher bench.

A lying cable curl works the biceps of Deborah Diana.

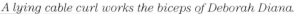

Incline dumbbell curls show off
Carla Dunlap's massive arms.

Standing Dumbbell Curl
Overall Biceps
(8–10 reps each set)

Adopt a comfortable standing position with your feet
about 12 inches (30 cm)
apart. Hold the dumbbells
in both hands and curl them
simultaneously until the
dumbbells are next to your shoulders. Start
with your palms facing your legs. When you
raise the weights turn your wrists so that the
palms are facing upwards. Lower the bells
slowly and repeat.

Shelley Gruwell does a single-arm curl.

Preacher Bench Curl
Overall Biceps
(8–12 reps each set)

Adopt a position with your
arms over a preacher
bench. Hold either a barbell
(as shown) or a pair of
dumbbells. Curl up to the
chin, then lower slowly. Do
not bounce the weights when the arms are in
the straight position. Raise and repeat. You
can change the angle of most preacher
benches to throw the stress on different areas
of the biceps.

Cable curls are demonstrated by Rachel McLish.

Forearm Exercises

Preacher Bench Wrist Curl
Forearm Flexors
(10–15 reps each set)

Adopt a position with your arms over a preacher bench as illustrated, restricting the movement to the wrists. Curl the hands in a deliberate and forceful manner. Concentrate the action of the exercise into your lower arms.

Behind-back Wrist Curl
Forearm Flexors
(12–15 reps each set)

Place a barbell behind the back as illustrated, facing directly to the front. Proceed to raise the hands rearwards and upwards. Restrict all movements to the hands and wrists only.

Reverse Curl
Forearm Extensors
(12–15 reps each set)

Stand erect, holding a barbell slightly wider than shoulder width. Allow the arms to hang down straight, elbows at your side, hands gripped with knuckles up. As your curl the barbell, keep your wrists straight and level with your forearms, elbows tucked in. Lower and repeat. You will feel this exercise in the upper forearm, near the elbow.

Wrist Curl
Forearm Belly
(12–15 reps each set)

Wrist curls work the flexors (the belly) of the forearm. Perform them in a seated position, with your lower arms resting on your knees (palms up) or on the top of a bench. Your hands must be unobstructed. Some top women keep their elbows close, while others allow their elbows to be comfortably apart—from 10–16 inches (25–40 cm).

Moving only your wrists, curl the weight upwards, until your forearms are fully contracted. Allow the barbell to lower under control.

Reverse Wrist Curl
Forearm Extensors
(12–15 reps each set)

This exercise is performed in the same manner as the regular wrist curl, but your palms should face downwards instead of upwards. Most people find it more comfortable to keep the arms at least 12 inches (30 cm) apart in this variation. You will use considerably less weight in this exercise than in the regular wrist curl.

WAISTLINE TRIMMING

Inger Zetterqvist

Shaping Your Abs

The first point to make clear on the subject of abdominal muscles is that if you have a moderate or thick layer of fat around your waist, you will not be able to get your abdominal muscles to show up sharply by merely performing a few sit-ups and leg raises. In fact, no amount of waistline exercises will work. The abdominals are developed, like any other muscle group, with progressive-resistance exercise. And like any other area they are defined by putting the body into a negative calorie balance until virtually all the superfluous fat is reduced.

There is no direct link between abdominal exercises and fat reduction around the waist area, other than the amount of calories burned in the execution of that exercise. However, burned-up fat will be lost from all over the body rather than specifically around the midsection. A three-mile walk will do more to help your waistline than several sets of ab exercises. The walk burns more calories. All the top bodybuilders know that abdominals are *built* with quality waist exercise and *honed* with diet and aerobic activity.

Have you noticed that some women have stomach muscles that have straight, lined-up ridges, while others appear to have more inconsistent, uneven abs? The shape that you have now cannot change. True, you can trim down or build up your muscularity, but you cannot alter the formation of your stomach muscles. Nor should an uneven ab formation

Crunches fully contract the abs of Cory Everson.

count against you in competition. A well-conditioned waistline is what counts the most.

There is a controversy about exercising the abdominal muscles. Joe Weider, Vince Gironda, and other noted experts have pointed out that the abdominals require no more than 8–12 repetitions for maximum growth and tone, and that more repetitions are only a waste of time. Other experts, such as Bill Pearl, Candy Csencsits and Frank Zane, feel that high-repetition movements are more advantageous.

There is little doubt that both methods work. The question that arises is whether or not high repetitions are actually more effective than low reps.

It would be a fair recommendation to advise that you train using the method that suits your personality. If you feel more comfortable using less resistance with 100 or 200 reps per set, then carry on. From the other point of view, using reps in the 10–15 range (often using additional resistance) may be more to your liking. Bodybuilding pros like Rachel McLish and Gladys Portugues use 15–30 reps in most of their ab training.

If you haven't been doing many waist exercises lately, do not make the mistake of suddenly throwing yourself into a hectic ab workout. The midsection is extremely sensitive to overwork. It forms a nerve center of the body, and too much ab work too soon can throw your body functions for a loop. The shock can stifle the growth of muscle tissue all over the body, cause sleepless nights, and create an overtrained feeling of exhaustion. *Ease* your way into any new abdominal-training program if you want maximum results.

If you desire clear-cut, sharp abdominal muscles, you must think either in terms of diet, or of physically burning up more calories each day. The best and fastest method is to attack the problem on both fronts. Combine these two aspects with a variety of quality abdominal exercises and workouts and you will have all the waistline slenderness you could possibly desire.

Two additional tips. Never push your stomach out (even for a joke): It can overstretch the abdominal wall. Once this is done it cannot return to normal. You can liken the effect to a spring that is pulled out to a point beyond which it will spring back. The strain in the metal has caused a rupture and nothing will induce it to regain its elasticity. The wearing of a weightlifting belt during your workouts will help prevent "overstretch." The other tip is to avoid taking any type of thyroid or steroid drug because each can lead to a bloated waistline area as a side effect.

Here are the abdominal exercises.

Side Twist
Intercostals
(50–300 reps each set)

Not all bodybuilders believe in the effectiveness of this exercise. It does, however, mobilize the waist area, and the oblique muscles are worked quite strongly despite little or no resistance. Your ability to twist in certain poses will also be greatly facilitated. Perform high repetitions as you twist from side to side, and make a conscious effort not to turn your hips too much to either side.

Partial Sit-up
Entire Abdominal Wall
(8–15 reps each set)

Lie on the floor or on a flat bench with your knees raised. You may either cross your ankles or hold your feet together. Holding your hands behind your head, at-tempt to raise your shoulders from the floor while drawing your knees towards your face. Lower your shoulders and legs simultaneously.

Seated Bent-knee Raise
Frontal Abdominals
(15–20 reps each set)

Adopt a position on a flat exercise bench as illustrated. Hold the bench to establish and fix your body at the correct angle. Raise the knees up to the chest and then straighten out the legs towards the ground. Keep the stress on the waist area by holding your position until the end of the exercise.

Diana Dennis performs leg raises for her abdominals.

Lisa Lyon illustrates the technique for doing partial sit-ups.

Hanging Leg Raise
**Lower Abdominals
(12–25 reps each set)**

Hang from an overhead horizontal bar, with your arms about 20 inches (50 cm) apart. Keeping your legs straight, raise them until they are just past the parallel-to-floor position. Lower and repeat. Try not to let the body build up a swinging motion.

For those who are unable to perform this exercise with straight legs, start off with the knees bent. Tuck your knees into the waist at each repetition, and point your toes downwards. Start the raise slowly, with positively no swinging. After a few weeks you will be able to graduate to the straight-leg style.

Shelley Gruwell demonstrates the bench crunch exercise.

Side Bend
Obliques
(15 + reps each set)

Stand in the upright position, feet comfortably apart, toes pointing slightly outward. Bend with a forceful effort to first one side and then the other. When your body is used to this movement you may hold a dumbbell in one hand. This works the opposite side to which you are holding the weight. After the allocated number of repetitions, hold the dumbbell in the other hand and repeat.

Roman Chair Sit-up
Lower and Middle Abdominals
(10–25 reps each set)

You need a Roman chair to anchor your legs in position and allow the trunk to sink completely down, thus working the abdominal region to a greater degree. Perform this with a steady rhythm and no bouncing. This is a favorite exercise of many pro bodybuilders who use it to define their frontal abdominal muscles.

Bench Crunch
Middle and Upper Abdominals
(10–15 reps each set)

Lie on your back on the floor. Your calves should rest on a bench in such a way that your thighs are vertical. Place your hands behind your head and *slowly* attempt to sit up. Because of the fixed position of the legs the maximum contraction is not passed over as in the regular sit-up movement (not recommended). There is constant tension in the middle and upper abdominals.

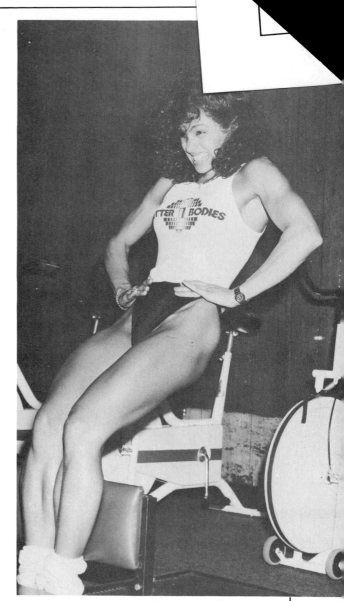

Roman chair sit-ups really tax the abs of Gladys Portugues.

Bent-over Twist
Side and Intercostal Areas
(30 + reps each set)
Start by getting into the position as illustrated. Hold a bar or a broomstick behind your head against your shoulders. This serves to increase and facilitate your twisting motion. Twist deliberately to either side while holding your basc position.

SHOULDERS

The press behind neck pumped up by Rachel McLish.

Building Delightful Delts

Shoulder width and deltoid size used to be the exclusive domain of males. Ten years ago, you couldn't interest many women in developing a firm, muscular shoulder region. In those yesteryears, the line from a woman's ears had to slope delicately to the shoulder region. Certainly a deltoid was just *not* part of a woman's anatomy.

Today we have millions of women who want well-developed delts to enhance their own physiques. Delts are delightful. Just as they set up a man's physique, they also add to a woman's appearance.

The deltoids are a three-headed muscle positioned at the end of your collarbone. Basically, it has three distinct functions: to raise the arm forward, sideward, and backwards.

It is true that you need to work your shoulders from different angles in order to bring out a complete-looking development, but do not carry this idea too far. Deltoids can be overtrained and injuries can occur. Without proper rest and good exercise form, you could sustain ligament, tendon, or even rotator cuff injuries. The latter comes from heavy jerk-type pressing, without adequate warm-ups.

If you have naturally wide shoulders, you will not have to work very hard to be impressive in that area. Women with narrow shoulders, however, must work very hard,

A dumbbell lateral raise is performed by Julie McNew.

Debbie Duncanson pumps up her rear deltoids on a machine.

building the delts from every angle, particularly the lateral (side) head, which gives the most width to the body.

The injury factor can also come about if you change from working one deltoid to the other without a proper warm-up. For example, if you were doing heavy bench-presses for the chest and then picked up a pair of heavy dumbbells for standing lateral raises for the shoulders, you could tear a muscle. The bench presses put enormous strain on the front deltoid, and then to suddenly switch to all-out side deltoid work is not wise. Of course, it does not just happen by combining these two exercises. You could pull a muscle following *any* combination. When attacking a complicated area such as the deltoids (with its three distinct heads) always begin each different movement using a light-to-medium warm-up weight first. *It allows the fibres and tendons time to adjust to the new direction of stress.*

Here are the shoulder exercises.

Shelley Gruwell

*Rachel McLish
demonstrates the cable lateral raise.*

Standing Dumbbell Press
Front and Side Shoulders
(8–10 reps each set)

While in the standing position as shown, hold two
dumbbells at the shoulders.
Keep your back straight and
your head up. Press both
dumbbells simultaneously
to the overhead position. Do not lean backwards during the exercise. Lower and repeat
with a steady rhythm.

Lateral Raise
Side Deltoids
(8–12 reps each set)

There are a thousand and
one ways to perform this
exercise, all with one purpose—to throw the stress
onto the side deltoids. Perform this exercise standing
upright, feet apart, or seated on the end of a
bench, feet flat on the floor together. Arms
must be bent or almost at right angles to
throw stress on the all-important lateral deltoids. Raise the weights from the straight-arm
position to level with your head, and immediately lower. Keep palms facing downwards
throughout. At the time of peak effort, try and
lean forward, rather than rearwards (which
will again put stress on the powerful front deltoids).

Upright Row
Side Deltoids
(8–15 reps each set)

Use a fairly wide grip. The wider the grip the more stress is put on the side deltoids. A narrow grip will put more effort on the frontal deltoids and the trapezius. Always straighten the arms at the bottom of the exercise, and start your pull slowly, gathering momentum as the weight rises to your chin area. Keep the up-down movement rhythmic. Maintain an upright stance with feet comfortably apart. As the bar rises, try to keep your elbows as high as possible, and do not lean backwards.

Gladys Portugues works her deltoids with wide-grip upright rows.

Mohamed Makkawy spots Gladys Portugues as she does face-down flyes.

Incline Face-down Flye
Rear Deltoids
(12–15 reps each set)

Sit face down on an incline bench, set at about a 35–40-degree angle. Holding two light dumbbells, raise the arms up and down, tilting them slightly forward as if you were pouring from a pitcher. The arms should be unlocked at the elbows rather than straight to alleviate pressure on the elbows. Do not swing the arms upwards. Start slowly and force the rear deltoids to *lift* the weight.

Standing Barbell Press
Front and Side Shoulders
(8–12 reps each set)

Stand with your feet comfortably apart as illustrated. Holding the barbell at your shoulders, press the weight straight upwards, being careful not to lean backwards excessively as the bar rises. Lock the arms briefly at the top of the movement. Lower and repeat.

Press behind Neck
Side Deltoids
(6–12 reps each set)

Sit down on a special upright bench with supports, and hold a loaded barbell above your head with your hands spaced moderately wide apart. Lower the weight as far as possible behind the neck, and immediately raise it when the b[...] your trapezius. Do not bounce th[...] your shoulders. Keep your elbows as far back as possible throughout the movement. Lock the elbows as the arms extend overhead, but do not hold the position. Continue pressing upwards and downwards, rhythmically without pause.

Alternate Dumbbell Press
Side Deltoids
(8–12 reps each set)

Sit on a flat bench holding a pair of dumbbells at the shoulders, palms facing inward or forward. Hold elbows back to maintain stress on your side deltoids. Start with your weakest hand, and alternately press first one dumbbell and then the other in a see-saw fashion. Lock the arm each time you press the weight, but do not maintain the straight-arm position. Lower and continue the exercise with no pauses.

Note the definition in Mary Roberts's shoulders as she does bent-over laterals.

THE HOURGLASS FIGURE

Carla Dunlap widens her amazing back with wide-grip pulldowns.

Backing Into Shape

"Muscles," says Rachel McLish, "should complement a woman's body from every angle and in every attitude of her physical being."

The hourglass figure is still very much a part of women's bodybuilding, and a strong, tapered back is part of an hourglass figure.

There are several controversies surrounding back training that we should bring to your attention. The first is the question of whether wide-grip chins and pulldowns are comparable to narrow- or medium-grip pulldowns and chins.

The argument is that the lat muscle is worked over a wider range when a narrow grip is used instead of a wide grip. The same argument, of course, is used with regard to the standing press and the popular bench press. Medium-grip usage maximizes the involvement of the delts (in pressing), the pecs (in benching), and the lats (in chinning), but there is a compensatory and *unwanted* involvement of the arms. The biceps and triceps are taking on more of the work.

In view of the fact that virtually all bodybuilders (male and female) renowned for their wide and dramatic V-shaped backs have used wide-grip chins and pulldowns in their training, it is suggested that you experiment in this area for yourself.

All back work interrelates one area with another, yet there are selective parts that require individual attention. To simplify things, we would be fairly safe in stating that the width of the back (the flair or V-shape) is built with pulldowns and chins, the thickness of the back is created mostly from T-bar rows and floor pulley rows, and hyperextensions are responsible for the lower-back development.

The trapezius, the muscle between the neck and the shoulders, is also considered a back muscle, because it covers most of the middle part of the upper back. It is worked with shrug exercises and all rowing and pulley motions.

Women, unless they can do more than 20 reps of chinning, should *never* hang weights from the body to add resistance. This encourages too much use of the arms instead of the lats. Weight should only be added when you can execute and maintain perfect "elbows-back" smooth chins from the beginning to end of your set.

Here are the exercises.

This well-shaped back belongs to Lisa Kolakowski.

T-Bar Row
Lower Lats
(8–12 reps each set)

This movement, primarily for the belly of the latissimus, is performed on a special apparatus, and it is almost identical to the bent-over barbell rowing motion, except that one end of your lever bar is anchored to the floor. As a result of this, there may be less strain on the lower back. Raise the weight upwards and downwards smoothly. Stretch out the arms (straight) at the bottom of the movement. Keep your back straight throughout the exercise.

Prone Hyperextension
Lower Back
(10–20 reps each set)

This is performed on an exercise unit especially designed for the job. Until recently, it was performed from a high bench or table. Place your legs and hips front downwards on a suitable table top. A training partner should hold your legs down to prevent your falling off the end. Your upper body should be free to bend upwards and downwards. Hold your hands behind your head. There is no need to bring the body up beyond being parallel to the floor.

Prone hyperextensions are good for the lower back.

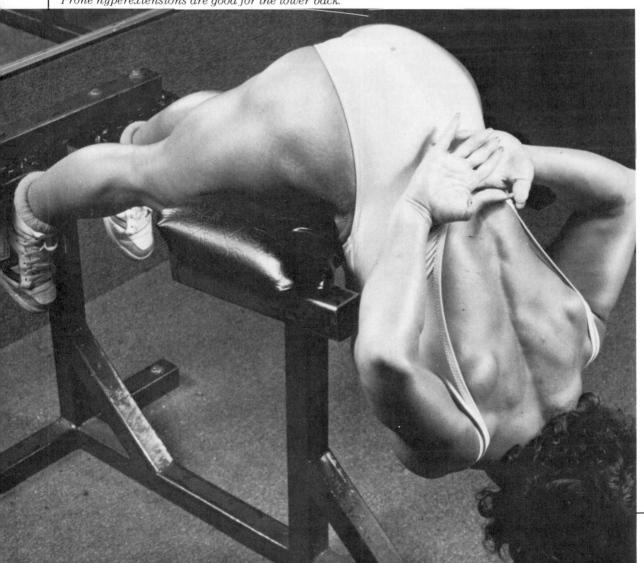

Wide-grip Chin
Lat Width
(8–15 reps each set)

Grasp an overhead bar using an overgrip (palms down) at least a foot wider than your shoulders on either side. (If your shoulders are 16 inches (40 cm) across, take a grip about 40 inches (100 cm) wide.) Pull upwards, keeping your elbows *back* throughout the movement. You may pull up so that the bar is either in front of or behind your neck. Some women like to change around for variety, but it would not be correct to say that one form is superior to the other. Lower until your arms are straight and repeat.

The good-morning exercise works the lower back.

Parallel-grip chins are performed by Mary Roberts.

Good-Morning Exercise
Lower Back
(10–15 reps each set)

Stand with your legs set comfortably, a loaded barbell across your shoulders. Keeping your back straight, bend forward at the waist and straighten up. Hold your head as high as you can throughout the movement. You may want to wrap a towel around the bar to prevent chafing at the neck.

Single-arm rowing—Lori Bowen-Rice shows how.

Single-arm Dumbbell Row
Middle Lats
(8–12 reps each set)

Another total lat exercise, but one that eliminates lower-back strain, since your free arm is used to support the entire upper body. Pull the dumbbell up into the midsection, and lower until the arm is extended all the way down, and then try a little harder to lower it even more. Maximize the stretch.

Incline Dumbbell Row
Overall Lat
and Upper Back
(8–12 reps each set)

Adopt a position on an incline bench as illustrated. Holding a dumbbell in either hand, pull upwards with a strong rowing motion. Lower slowly until the arms are completely straight in the down position. Raise and lower with an even rhythm.

Parallel-grip Pulldown
Lat Belly
(10–15 reps each set)

A pulldown or lat machine is required for this. Use a parallel-grip bar while seated at a lat machine. Pull the bar downwards from the arms-straight-overhead position until it is touching the upper chest. Allow the bar to pull back upwards and repeat the movement. Keep your back straight during the exercise.

Overgrip Chin
Lower Lats
(8–15 reps each set)

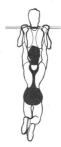

Using a standard overhead chinning bar, grab it with a fairly close grip, palms facing forward. Start by hanging so that the arms are straight. Begin the pullup or chin with a slow, concentrated effort. Do not jerk or jump up from the floor. Raise until your chin is above the level of the bar; lower under control and repeat.

Rachel McLish exhibits super form in the low-pulley rowing exercise.

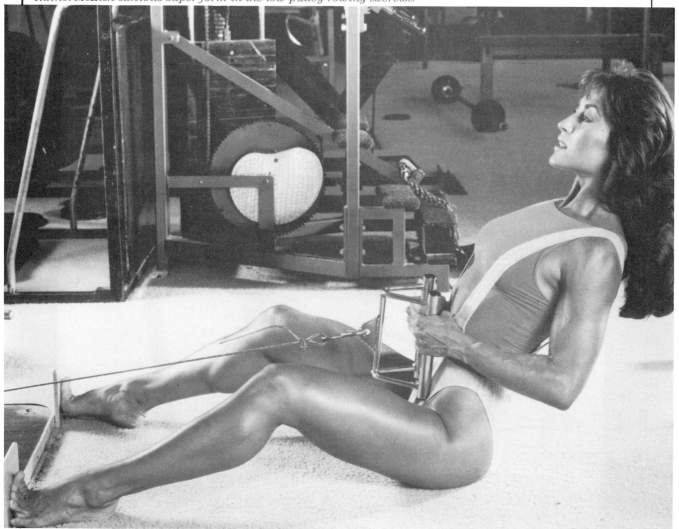

Britain's Carolyn Cheshire puts the lat machine to good use.

Mary Roberts demonstrates the close-grip pulldown.

Lat-machine Pulldown
V-shape Development
(10–15 reps each set)

This exercise has to be performed on a lat machine. Take a wide overgrip on the bar, and pull down as far as you can. This exercise is not as effective as the wide-grip chinning exercise, but it does have the advantage that you can use less resistance and pull the bar lower, working your lats over a greater range of movement. You may pull to the front or the back of the neck.

Close-Grip Pulldown
Lower Lats
(10–15 reps each set)

Again, you will need a lat machine for this exercise. All modern gyms have a least one of these as a standard piece of equipment. Pull the bar down to the front of the chest as shown, tensing your back as you do so. Allow the arms to straighten and repeat. Do not jerk rearwards as you pull the weight downwards.

Lori Bowen-Rice illustrates the stiff-legged deadlift—a variation on the regular exercise.

Deadlift
Lower and Overall Back
(5–10 reps each set)

Bend over a loaded barbell with your feet comfortably apart. Grip the barbell with one hand under and the other hand over the bar (about shoulder width).

Straighten the back, bend the knees, and pull the bar upwards as you straighten to a standing position. Keep your head up throughout the exercise. Lower and repeat. Do not bounce the weight on the floor.

BODYBUILDING PRINCIPLES

Lori Bowen-Rice

A Scientific Art

Weight training does not just involve *lifting weights*. It has developed into a scientific practice involving many complex principles and theories. Today this art is quite sophisticated, and as time goes on and the body's feedback mechanisms are more identi-

Julie McNew

fiable (and transferable to computer language) we will probably get even more scientific.

Bodybuilders have been using their own training "secrets" for scores of years, each method developed from preceding ones. Almost every book or magazine publisher brought out a different system. Peary Rader, publisher of *Iron Man*, presented the Rader method of training, while Bob Hoffman of the York Barbell Company produced the York courses. Even the old Milo Barbell Company had its own training methods.

However, it was Joseph Weider who put much time into organizing the various principles into comprehensive training methods. After sifting through the exercise routines of the successful bodybuilding champions, certain patterns of training emerged. Over the years, Joe Weider selectively adopted some techniques, some of which he modified, and threw out others. Most importantly, each technique had to be publicized, developed and perfected, and, of course, updated on a regular basis. Through regular promotion, a number of exercise standards now exist, many of which the bodybuilding world knows best and recognizes as Weider principles.

Joe Weider was so successful in publicizing these techniques and principles that many people naturally assumed he was the originator of them all. The bottom line, of course, was that Joe Weider didn't claim to have *invented* all the various systems. He merely adopted a brand name for those techniques which he felt were representative of his personal training philosophy. But to give the California publisher his due, there are more than a few cases where fully crystallized Weider principles were born from very obscure sources. In other words, if it were not for Joe Weider's involvement in developing many of the principles we now take for granted, they would not exist in their present-day identifiable form.

Here are a few of the more popular and workable systems.

Straight Sets

For all its simplicity, the straight set system has continued to be used by more weight trainers than any other method. Straight sets simply imply that a trainer performs a series of repetitions (a set) of a particular exercise, pauses for 30–90 seconds, and then resumes additional sets of the same exercise, allowing for subsequent rests between each set. Generally speaking, the number of sets per exercise is between three and five.

Should the exerciser choose to perform another movement for the same body part, it is usual to group the exercises for each body part together. For example, you would group all the chest exercises together, all the leg exercises, shoulders, biceps, triceps, and so forth.

Straight sets have been used for almost a century, but they have been used extensively only after World War II. Virtually every bodybuilder of renown has used this technique more than any other.

Heavy-Duty Training

This name has come to be synonomous with an exercise technique that pushes the body's capacity until the muscle being exercised actually *fails* in the completion of a repetition. Heavy-duty training is the logical way to train when one considers the scientific data compiled by orthodox medical findings (i.e.: that a muscle only grows when it is subjected to an ever-increasing workload).

The key word to this technique is *intensity*, which embodies excessive effort on behalf of the trainer. High-intensity techniques are employed for forced reps, negative resistance, pre-exháust, and rest-pause training. Because of the high degree of effort required in a heavy-duty set, the actual amount of sets in a typical heavy-duty program is only one or two per exercise.

The heavy-duty method has been used by almost every champion in one way or another. Although it has not been accepted universally by weight trainers, it has provided

Sue Ann McKean

excellent results to many bodybuilders throughout the world.

Supersets

All muscles contract and shorten, then return to their original length. The biceps muscle contracts and pulls the forearm upwards. The triceps muscle, in back of the arm, pulls the arm straight. Bodybuilders, however, call them pulling and pushing muscles.

Pushing exercises include the standing press, supine bench press, push-up, triceps extension, and leg press. Pulling exercises refer to upright row, curl, chin, bent-over row, and thigh curl.

The idea of supersets is to alternate two exercises rapidly without rest—one pulling and one pushing movement. It was common to alternate curls with triceps extensions, but many top bodybuilders would simply alternate two curling movements, two pectoral movements, or two triceps movements, not caring whether a particular muscle was being worked against another (for example, the biceps and triceps). Today, supersets merely refer to the alternation of two exercises in rapid succession.

This type of exercise can jolt the muscles into new growth in weeks, but it is very severe; too much could cause you to come to a standstill. Paradoxically, you can break a standstill with a week or two of supersetting your exercises.

Forced Negatives and Reps

When you cannot perform another repetition of an exercise you can call upon a training partner to assist the lift by giving a light touch to the bar as it is lifted. This is known as a *forced rep* because without the help you could not successfully complete the exercise.

The raising of a weight is known as *concentric contraction*, while the lowering of a weight (returning to starting position from the point of full contraction) is known as *eccentric contraction*.

Forced reps involve the help of another person in aiding the weight upwards. A *negative* rep is the eccentric contraction. It is not too difficult to see that it is often easier to lower a weight slowly (benefitting from the negative aspect) than it is to lift the weight upwards in the first instance.

Let's relate this to a practical example. Imagine you are performing a standing barbell curl. You manage eight good reps on your own (unassisted). Normally you would end the set there. You can further stress the muscle by having a training partner stand in front of you, using a finger to get the weight up while you perform yet another curl (forced rep). Then you can compound the effect even more by lowering the weight slowly (negative rep).

It should be noted that negative reps are not suited to all. You have to have an exceptional capacity to "take it." Even the hardiest bodybuilders only practice negative reps for some of their exercises some of the time. Negative reps require more recuperation time and can lead to some mighty sore muscles if you are not used to heavy exercise, so take it easy when first trying this technique.

The Pre-Exhaust System

The pre-exhaust system is based on attacking a specific muscle with a carefully chosen isolation exercise, followed immediately by a combination movement.

Let's look at the chest muscles. In many chest exercises, are, for most people, the weakest link. In dips and bench and incline presses, the triceps are worked hard but the pectorals only moderately, so the triceps grow more rapidly than the chest. If you already have great pectoral muscles, it doesn't matter, but if you want to develop your pectorals, the pre-exhaust method will help.

To avoid using the triceps, isolate and exhaust the pecs first by doing an exercise where the triceps are not directly involved, such as dumbbell flyes. Performing the exercise to the point of failure, go right to a second exercise, such as the incline or bench press (combination movement).

After the presses, the triceps will temporarily be stronger than the pectorals, which are in a state of near exhaustion from the first isolation exercise. In other words, you need not be limited by the "weak link" triceps.

The following is a complete pre-exhaust routine showing exercise combinations for each area.

Shoulders
Isolation Movement
   Lateral Raise with Dumbbells
Combination Movement
   Press behind Neck or Upright Row

Chest
Isolation Movement
   Low Incline Flye or Cable Crossover
Combination Movement
   Medium-grip Bench Press or Incline Bench Press

Thighs
Isolation Movement
   Thigh Extension
Combination Movement
   Leg Press or Squat

Back
Isolation Movement
   Lat Shrugs on Parallel Bars (Keep arms straight throughout. Try to touch ears with shoulders.)
Combination Movement
   T-bar Row or Bent-over Row

Abdominals
Isolation Movement
   Crunches
Combination Movement
   Hanging Leg Raise

Calves
Isolation Movement
   Calf Raise
Combination Movement
   Rope Jumping

Biceps
Isolation Movement
   Preacher Bench Curl
Combination Movement
   Narrow-undergrip Chin

Triceps
Isolation Movement
   Triceps Pressdown (on lat machine)
      or
   One-arm Triceps Stretch
Combination Movement
   Narrow-grip Bench Press
   (with hands 2
   inches [5 cm] apart)

Forearms
Isolation Movement
   Reverse Wrist Curl
Combination Movement
   Reverse Curl

Dr. Lynn Pirie

If you wish to split this routine so that you train four or five times a week working only half the schedule at one time, it is suggested that you work legs, back, and biceps one day, and chest, shoulders, triceps, and forearms on alternate days. The waist can be worked every day.

The amount of sets and reps you do is entirely up to you. Those new to pre-exhaust training should perhaps limit their sets to two. As your condition improves you may perform up to four sets of each exercise, but no more. Reps should average around ten. Some trainers will get best results doing sets of eight whereas others may get more from utilizing a scheme of twelve reps or even more. Many women only use the pre-exhaust system on one or two exercises in their schedule, electing to use straight sets or other variations for the balance of their training routines.

Rest-Pause Training

This method has been used since the invention of barbells. Rest-pause training is not a system to be followed all the time, but it does permit you to greatly increase tendon and muscle strength and add to overall size in a few weeks, if that is what you want.

It's a simple idea. After warming up for a particular exercise, load up the barbell sufficiently to allow for just one repetition. Let's assume you are doing a bench press: Press out one difficult rep and replace the bar on the stands. Allow 10–20 seconds to elapse and perform another repetition. After a similar brief rest, perform yet another repetition—and so on. Each time allow your body to partially recuperate. It's possible that you may have to reduce the weight slightly as the reps accumulate.

Peripheral Heart Action (PHA) Training

Developed by physical educator Bob Gadja in the 1960s, Peripheral Heart Action (PHA) training calls for the performance of one exercise for each major body part with a minimum of rest for four to six different areas. As you progress from one exercise to another, select movements which work totally unrelated areas. You would not, for example, perform a bench press, then a standing press, followed by dips, and arm movements.

A typical PHA series covers the whole body, from one extremity to another, such as from press behind neck to front squat to barbell curl to calf raise. In this way the blood does not become congested in one area. Growth still takes place, but truth to tell, it may not be as effective in creating muscle stimulation as other more forceful methods. But PHA is a *healthy* way to train. It incorporates progressive resistance (you add weight when you can). It utilizes time to advantage since there is no need for rest periods of any length because you are not waiting for a muscle area to partially recover before working it again.

The general procedure in setting up a PHA routine is to select four or six exercises for totally different body parts and place them into "cycles." The entire routine would then consist of two, three, or four cycles of four to six exercises each cycle. When you start your cycle you first perform exercise number one, then exercise number two, three, and so on. At the end of the first cycle you are permitted a two-minute rest, after which you start at the beginning of that same cycle again.

Important: Beginners should perform only one or two rotations of each cycle. Intermediates can perform three rotations of each cycle. Advanced trainers may perform up to five rotations of each cycle.

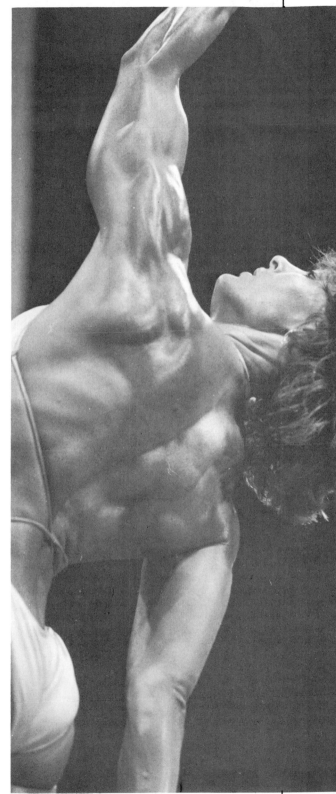

Lori Bowen-Rice

Lisa Kolakowski

Beginner's Routine

(Perform one or two rotations of each cycle only.)

Cycle One

Bench Press	10 reps
Barbell Curl	10 reps
Squat	12 reps
Seated Press behind Neck	12 reps

Cycle Two

Bent-over Row	10 reps
Calf Raise (Standing)	10 reps
Incline Sit-up	20 reps
Straight-arm Pullover	12 reps
Triceps Stretch (Lying)	10 reps

Intermediate Routine

(Perform three rotations of each cycle.)

Cycle One

Press behind Neck	8 reps
Squat	10 reps
Chin behind Neck	12 reps
Bench Press	8 reps

Cycle Two

Thigh Extension	12 reps
Hanging Leg Raise	20 reps
Calf Raise	20 reps
Barbell Curl	8 reps

Cycle Three

Incline Flye	10 reps
Thigh Curl	15 reps
Roman Chair Sit-up	20 reps
Triceps Stretch (Lying)	10 reps

Advanced Routine

(Perform three to five rotations.)

Cycle One

Standing Dumbbell Press	6 reps
Chin behind Neck	12 reps
Front Squat (feet on three-inch block)	10 reps
Wide-grip Bench Press	8 reps

Cycle Two

Roman Chair Sit-up	25 reps
Calf Raise	20 reps
Bent-over Row	10 reps
Incline Bent-arm Flye	10 reps

Cycle Three

Incline Leg Raise	20 reps
Barbell Curl	10 reps
Donkey Calf Raise	25 reps
Standing Triceps Stretch	10 reps

Cycle Four

Thigh Extension	12 reps
Incline Dumbbell Curl	10 reps
Standing Lateral Raise	10 reps
Lying Triceps Stretch	10 reps

Giant Sets

Sometimes known as *compound training*, a giant set is an advanced technique for exercising or shocking your muscles. An example of a giant set working the biceps would be to perform three or four biceps exercises, one after the other in rotation, with minimal rest between each exercise. You might do:

Barbell Curl 10 reps

Incline Dumbbell Curl 10 reps

Seated Dumbbell Curl 10 reps

Preacher Bench Curl 10 reps

After you have performed one set of each of the above, go back again to the beginning and perform another cycle of rotation. You may do two, three, or even four cycles of these giant sets, bearing in mind, of course, that four cycles would give you a total of 16 sets overall for the biceps. This is definitely *advanced* training.

Muscle-Priority System

This is one of the oldest Weider principles of all, one that has been highly promoted in *Muscle & Fitness* magazine and its predecessor *Muscle Builder*.

It is a well-known fact that you are freshest and have more vigor and energy at the beginning of a workout. Consequently, it would make sense to work those body parts which are in most need of attention—first.

If you have weak, underdeveloped shoulders, for example, perform all your shoulder work *first* in your workout while you have the best mental drive and fresh energy to do maximum justice to the area. This may sound very basic, but you would be surprised at how many bodybuilders work their best areas first and their least-responsive body parts last. This is the exact opposite to the philosophy behind the muscle-priority principle.

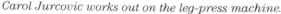

Carol Jurcovic works out on the leg-press machine.

Peak Contraction

Very few bodybuilding exercises allow for full resistance to be placed on a muscle when it is completely contracted. For example, when you do a barbell curl the hardest part of the movement is when the forearms are parallel to the floor. After that point has been passed the completion of the movement becomes easier. Peak contraction is the term used to describe those movements where the hardest part of an exercise coincides with the muscle being fully flexed at its conclusion. As Joe Weider says in his book *Competitive Bodybuilding*: "To get the most out of an exercise, you should have a heavy weight on a working muscle when the largest number of muscle cells have been fired off."

The peak-contraction training principle keeps stress on the muscle when it is fully contracted. Some of these exercises are: 90-degree Scott curls, incline or standing leg curls, leg extensions, hyperextensions, shrugs, calf raises, upright rows, bent-over rows, pulldowns, side laterals, dumbbell kickbacks, crunches, bent-over laterals, front barbell and dumbbell laterals, supine dumbbell curls, hanging leg raises, and inversion boot sit-ups.

When you employ peak-contraction exercises you should consciously hold the fully contracted position of each repetition for two or three seconds to engage all the muscle fibres to the maximum.

Pyramid Training

Pyramid training is used by pro bodybuilders more than any other principle. It involves adding weight and decreasing repetitions each successive set. After your heaviest weight has been used, there is a corresponding reduction (or stripping) in weight each set as you gradually work down. The pyramid method is almost always used in the squat and bench press exercises. Here's how a particular pyramid set might work out for you in the squat.

Erika Mes

Set 1	40 lbs., 20 reps
Set 2	80 lbs., 12 reps
Set 3	100 lbs., 10 reps
Set 4	120 lbs., 8 reps
Set 5	130 lbs., 6 reps
Set 6	100 lbs., 15 reps
Set 7	80 lbs., 20 reps

Looking at the above, you can probably figure out that the first two sets are little more than warm-ups for the three sets that follow.

We have now covered all the major bodybuilding principles and exercises that you should know—whether you are just getting started or are determined to become a top contender in this exciting new sport for women. Just how far you wish to go is entirely up to you!

GETTING RIPPED

Gladys Portugues

Contest Preparation

Getting "ripped" is a process whereby a bodybuilder reduces her body-fat level to the extent that the muscles show to a maximum effect in preparation for a contest. This is primarily done with diet and aerobic exercise. Your actual weight-training schedule should include more isolation exercises than you normally would use during the off-season training period. As contest time approaches, your exercises can be performed with increased intensity with somewhat less rest between sets.

How low should the body-fat percentage go? Most winners of modern bodybuilding contests weigh in at 8–12 percent body fat. You will hear of lower percentages, but these are seldom documented.

One of the mistakes of contest preparation is to start dieting too late and too drastically. As we suggested earlier, an extreme reduction in calories can put your system into shock and actually set off a physiological alarm, directing the body to rebel and retain fat cells. The extreme starvation, or near starvation, will cause your metabolic rate to quickly compensate for the "coming famine" by shutting down all systems not necessary for life. Calories are stored and you become smoother—the opposite effect of what you want.

Carolyn Cheshire, Britain's number-one professional bodybuilder and a woman noted for her ability to get ripped, says:

> I never starve myself before a show. Four months before a show, such as the IFBB Ms. Olympia, I reduce my calories slightly. At this stage I am only eight or nine pounds over by best contest weight. I just do not believe in bulking (fattening) up. I take those eight pounds off at the rate of just eight ounces a week (two pounds a month) and I believe this is the only sensible way to reduce.
>
> For the last four months I steadily left all the obvious fat out of my diet. I ate five meals a day, always including broiled chicken, white fish, and cottage cheese for protein. For carbohydrates I ate at least two baked potatoes, whole-wheat bread, vegetables, and fruit.

It should be pointed out that Carolyn's diet is extremely high grade. Natural foods

Carolyn Cheshire

Rachel McLish

only—no junk. She could eat in this way because she was:

- Not trying to lose a great deal of weight.
- Training extremely hard (six days a week on a three-day split routine).
- Incorporating an aerobics program of running or cycling (30–60 minutes) on a stationary bike two or three times a week.

The average woman is reputed to have about 22–26 percent body fat while a man has about 12–16 percent. A woman who lowers her percentage down to 10–12 percent will look extremely muscular. Australia's Bev Francis looked ripped to shreds in the Las Vegas Grand Prix, with a body fat percentage of 9 percent. Susie Green, a model turned bodybuilder, achieved a remarkable 4–6 percent body fat. The lowest figure we can recall at this time was taken from Debbie Basile, the American women's lightweight champion, who was hydrostatically weighed (the method of reading how much bodyweight is lean and how much is fat) at an amazing 4.07 percent. Still, is less actually better? A low body fat is an important factor for winning a contest, but if you go too low, there is the possibility of appearing stringy and emaciated, both of which detract from the likelihood of the judging panel awarding you a first-place trophy.

A woman's menstrual cycle is disrupted (stops) when her body fat goes below 10 percent. This absence of periods (amenorrhea) is merely nature's precaution against a woman getting pregnant when she doesn't appear to have the means (nutritional supply) to support the healthy growth of a fetus.

"Amenorrhea is not permanent, and there is no evidence to show that it is harmful to the female reproductive system," concluded the American College of Sports Medicine from a 1979 study after recognizing the fact that many female athletes had menstrual irregularities as a result of achieving low body-fat levels.

When you reduce your body-fat level the breasts will also lose considerable size (being primarily made up of fat cells). This, of course, is not just applicable to bodybuilders, but virtually all athletes. A highly fit and physically efficient state precludes the necessity of full breast size, and during peak conditioning women will have a minimum of breast adipose.

One of the dietary enemies of bodybuilding at contest-cutting time is salt. Table salt is the biggest offender, but if you study labels you will be surprised at how much there is in prepared foods.

Rachel McLish readily admits that when she's dieting for a contest she will be quite liberal with her salt intake. It is during the last four or five days that Rachel will *absolutely* stop all salt intake in order to avoid any water retention at contest time. By her own admission, Ms. McLish admits that if she tries to keep salt out of her diet for more than a few days, weeks, or even months, then even the smallest indiscretion or slip can result in a high degree of water retention.

Carolyn Cheshire agrees with this philosophy, as does Gladys Portugues, Erika Mes, Julie McNew, and others. You cannot avoid salt for too long a period.

Other contest-ripping techniques include sunbathing or spending time in a sauna. Laura Combes was one of the first bodybuilders to use sunbathing as part of her contest preparation. She felt it depleted water from under the skin. The important thing to remember about lying in the sun is that you do not overdo it. Too much sun drains you of energy.

The use of saunas as a means of losing water under the skin, sweating it out as it were, is becoming more popular. But there's a two-sided catch here. If you drink as much liquid as you've sweated' in the sauna, your body will simply gain back everything you lost in order to even up the balance. And on the other side of the coin, if you do not take in liquids at all, you run the risk of dehydration, and that can be a serious problem.

Diuretics are used by some women in order to induce the body to shed water via

Claire Furr

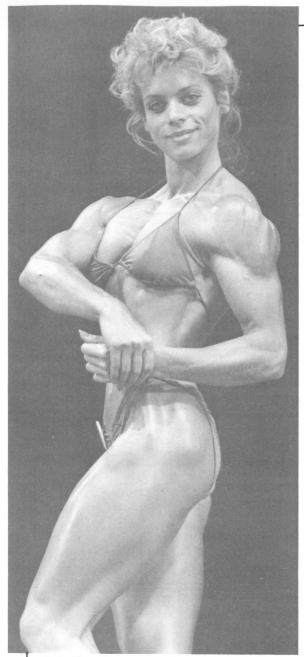

Carla Temple

body feedback principle is vitally important. You must monitor your energy levels and fat percentage daily. Use a pair of medical calipers to check the degree of subcutaneous fat (the thickness of your skin) at different sites on your body (i.e.: side of the waist, triceps, outer part of the upper thigh).

Bill Reynolds, who has co-authored several books for internationally known women bodybuilders, believes that it is a good idea to reward yourself while on a strict diet, with a healthy serving of high-fat foods every five or six days. "A couple of scoops of ice cream makes a perfect diversion," he says. "It will help you keep your sanity without wrecking your weight-loss momentum."

The final days of contest diet are usually hardest because you usually make that extra effort to restrict food intake, while still trying to maximize workout intensity so that muscle mass is not lost. At such times you will find yourself running out of steam in the middle of workouts and wondering if it is all worth it. During the last ten days, carbohydrates should also be reduced to an intake of not more than 60 grams daily, dropping down to about 30 grams daily for the last six days. Then for 24–36 hours prior to being judged you should increase carbohydrate consumption. This is known as carbohydrate loading (carbing up!). When it is correctly used, you will get full-looking muscles, sharp definition, muscularity, and a little vascularity.

Make sure that you carb up with complex carbohydrates, such as a baked potato or bran muffin rather than resort to sugar, fruit or ice cream. If you overload (eat too much), you run into the danger of accumulating excess water beneath the skin. Needless to say, liquid intake during the last two days should only be sufficient to quell your thirst on a short-term basis. It should be noted that some successful bodybuilders prefer to carb up slowly during the last three days prior to competition, rather than risk too much from a single binge the night before the show. This is a matter for your own experimentation.

excessive urination. This is definitely a dangerous practice since it can deplete potassium stores in the body. Potassium, among other things, is responsible for keeping your heart beat regular. Without it you could suffer cardiac arrest. Avoid using harsh drugstore products.

During the last two months prior to a contest, you will find yourself in a position of having to evaluate each and every day. This

Julie McNew puts an all-put effort into her contest preparation.

Pillow gives new meaning to the phrase getting ripped.

The Judging Process

The latest guidebook written by the International Federation of Bodybuilders sets the parameters for judging women's competitions:

In regard to muscular development, it must *not* be carried to excess where it resembles the massive muscularity of the male physique.

Definition of women's muscles must not be confused with emaciation, as the result of extreme loss of weight whereby the excessive loss of body fat reveals the underlying muscles which will then be flat, stringy and underdeveloped.

In Round Two, the judges may find other faults, such as stretch marks, operation scars, and cellulite. The judges shall also observe whether the women competitors walk to and from their positions in a graceful manner.

Women competitors must wear bikinis of a solid, non-distracting color, which should conform to accepted standards of taste and decency. The bikini must reveal the abdominal muscles as well as the lower-back muscles. The fastenings of the bikini must also be plain with no attached ornamentation. Metallic materials, such as gold or silver lamé, cannot be used to make up the bikini. Other rules include:

- Competitors must not wear footwear, watches, rings, bangles, pendants, earrings, wigs, distracting ornamentation, or artificial aids to the figure. They must not chew gum, eat candy, or smoke.
- Artificial body coloring may be used, provided that it is applied at least 24 hours prior to the prejudging.
- The excessive application of oil on the body is strictly forbidden, but body oils, skin creams, and moisturizers may be used in moderation.
- During the prejudging for women, the hair must be worn off the shoulders so as not to

Superbodybuilders Tony Pearson and Carla Dunlap

hide the musculature of the shoulders and upper back. The hair may be styled for the evening finals.

- The number issued by the judges's secretary to competitors must be pinned securely to the left side of the costume and must be worn during the prejudging and evening finals.

written criteria. If the titles are awarded to the biggest, most ripped competitors, we are not only encouraging the use of steroids by women, but we will lose the essence of what female bodybuilding is all about—healthy, ideal *womanhood*. Women *are* different from men, and it is this difference that they should nurture and take pride in. To aspire to mas-

Carla Dunlap, Cory Everson, Rachel McLish, Inger Zetterqvist, and Marjo Selin line up for a recent Ms. Olympia competition.

In spite of the clear IFBB rules, it is sometimes dismaying to find that the judges award a title to someone who does not fit the culinity is to put men in the position of being role models for women's physical perfection. This is most definitely not the way to go!

Gladys Portugues

Contest Dos and Don'ts

Do make sure that you start your diet well in advance of the contest. Three or four months is usually required. It is impractical to cut calorie consumption drastically in the hope of getting into top shape in a week or two.

Do get a good natural tan in the months leading up to a contest. Make sure you tan evenly, including under your arms. Most women also use artificial tanning makeup, which is applied daily during the last week or two before a contest. Build up layers of tanning makeup to get an overall dark tan.

Do be totally prepared for a show. Take along a sweatsuit, sneakers, two costumes, tanning lotion for last-minute touch-ups, towel, oil, shower slippers, stage pass, and your makeup and grooming kit.

Do not enter a contest unless you are ready for it. Attend several contests before you enter one as a competitor to learn what is expected of you. If you compete at a level way above your head, you will only feel foolish and possibly embarrassed.

Do not compete in too many contests. You can only peak two or three times a year at the most. An overabundance of contests could burn you out.

Do not cover your body with excessive amounts of oil. Apply vegetable oil (almond or avocado), not a petroleum-based oil, which will appear too reflective. Vegetable oil sinks into the skin. Do not compete without any oil.

Do not pump up excessively (floor dips, chins, light dumbbell work). This will flatten

Dinah Anderson

Erika Mes

out your physique. Merely perform a few exercises to get the blood circulating so you can feel your muscles. Only work those areas that need a little more size. Do not pump up your legs. It will interfere with your sensitivity for posing and no visible difference will be noticed from your efforts.

Do not get into arguments with officials or other competitors backstage. Do not strut around because you will be inviting verbal abuse from others. Do not use psychological tactics to psych-out the competition.

Be alive, alert, and ready. You are being looked at, assessed, and appraised onstage. Even when the judges are comparing other women, you should keep your muscles semi-tensed—you never know when a judge will be looking back at you. If you don't feel completely comfortable, *pretend* that you are. Be aware of directives from the head judge. Know your number as well as the order of the compulsory poses.

Smile when you're onstage. This is show business! Oh yes . . . and good luck!

Ben Weider presents the winners at a women's competition.

POSING

Ms. Olympia 1984 Cory Everson

Physical Charisma

When women began entering bodybuilding competitions en masse around 1978 they quickly upgraded the art of posing. The men had their eyes opened. Within a year every top male bodybuilder presented a better free-posing routine than he had ever managed before. But the women still lead the way.

On its lowest level, posing is simply a technique of presenting the muscles of the body for physical appraisal. But at its highest level it becomes a kinetic art form. Not only are the muscles shown to advantage, but the posing routine itself becomes an extension of the subject's personality. It is a finely constructed drama, with a beginning, middle, and end, all choreographed to inspiring music especially for the presentation.

A great posing routine is unforgettable. Your eyes feast upon it and the memory of the moment is locked into your mind. At the conclusion of an outstanding posing demonstration, an audience is moved, not only to rapturous applause, but to unadulterated adoration. Earth-shattering shouts and clapping acknowledge the champion as she leaves the stage.

Starting to pose may present a problem. Like anything else, you begin at the beginning—in front of your full-length mirror. Simply mimic the attitudes you see in the various muscle magazines. The more the better. Set up a double mirror so you can see your back at the same time. If you have a friend who can advise you, then so much the better. These early posing attempts will teach you about body awareness and muscle control. Both are essential if you are to enter a competition.

The next step is to attend physique contests. Watch how each contestant presents herself. Surprisingly, you may learn equally as much from the poor posers as you do from those who present themselves well.

It would be pointless to build a sensational body of just the right size, shape, and definition only to finish poorly in a contest because you failed to present your physique at its best. "Many women," says champion bodybuilder Laura Combes, "after slaving away for hundreds of hours in the gym, lose out at a contest because their posing is inept and ineffective."

Too many women practice only with a mirror, and as a result they look straight ahead on every pose. Of course, a mirror is good but don't let it dominate your style. Learn to pose without the mirror. One handy trick is to pose in front of the mirror with your

Gladys Portugues

175

Carla Temple

eyes closed, then after you have locked into the position, open your eyes to check the result. Another aid is to get someone to film your routine with a video camera. You can check over your faults time and time again, trying to improve each time.

Learn at least 15 poses for a good routine. Olympians can usually pull off 30 great poses, so try and aim for that. Remember that you will not be able to duplicate all the poses of the champions. Drop those that do not work for you, unless they happen to be some of the compulsory poses. All poses should be practiced; hold them for up to 30 seconds at a time. This will help your control and even improve your appearance in the poses you must perfect.

You may find it interesting to note that almost every top female bodybuilder has taught herself to pose. There are a few people who are experts on the subject of posing and are able to offer constructive advice, such as Art Zeller, Joe Weider, Vince Gironda, but most women learn first from the magazine pictures, then from viewing videotapes of the top contests or actually attending the contests.

It is a slow process, but expertise will come if you commit yourself to an attempt at progressive improvement. It all begins with imitation of others.

According to the IFBB judging system, there are five compulsory poses: These form Round One of the judging:

1. Front double biceps

2. Left-side chest

3. Back-double biceps

4. Right-side triceps

5. Front abdominals and thigh

Needless to say, you have to practice these poses regularly, especially when you are preparing for a contest. You can vary the poses slightly to fit your own physical makeup, but they cannot be changed much, otherwise the head judge will "call" you on it, and possibly deduct valuable points.

Round Two is the judging of your body in a relaxed position. Actually, of course, the body is anything but relaxed in this stance. Your lats are spread, the thighs and abdominals flexed, and you are prouder than a peacock! As Rachel "Ms. Flex Appeal" McLish says, "If you've ever seen a prima ballerina in action, you know that there is a difference between standing and *standing*!"

The third round is free posing. That is your individual posing routine with the emphasis on the word *your*! A free-posing routine is the stringing together of your best poses, using every trick in the book to win over the audience and judges. Only regular practice and commitment to excellence will perfect your free-posing routine.

You have to develop your optional poses, choose appropriate music, choreograph your program, and present it with an air of unshakable confidence and poise. Audience manipulation is your aim. Everyone in show business has to learn it. And this *is* show business. If this all sounds too much, then go back to basics—back to your full-length mirror. Take a cassette player with you and pose to your favorite music. Your routine will begin to emerge. Once you have got into "sliding" from one pose to another, you will be able to build a little more . . . gradually. One day you will have a routine.

Many bodybuilders actually have backgrounds in gymnastics (Lynn Conkwright) or

Mary Roberts

Marjo Selin

dance (Rachel McLish), both of which are very useful when it comes to posing. If you get stuck with the development of your posing routine, you could seek out a coach to help you. Hiring a dance choreographer may be a worthwhile investment. You could phone various dance studios listed in the yellow pages and explain what you would like to do. Make sure you agree on a fair fee for the service in advance. You will need several two- or three-hour sessions to formulate transitions (the way you move from one pose to another). Then you will have to practice for several weeks at home or in the gym.

Remember, the free-posing round is *you*. Unlike the compulsory rounds, no one is telling you what to do, how to stand, where to look. The free-posing round is the time to show all aspects of your body that you cannot display in the compulsory poses. You are aiming not only to show muscles and definition, but you are, if possible, to take the audience through an entire gamut of emotions. Never leave eye contact with your audience for more than one pose at a time. Use the shape of your body and the transitions between those shapes to *mesmerize* the crowd. Your total mastery must be experienced by the audience. During transitions, flex your muscles about 70 percent and as you lock into each pose go for broke. Ease off slightly if there is excessive shaking.

The music you choose must be part of the story. A pretty tune or an aggressive beat is *not* sufficient in itself. The music must suit your personality and the scope of your routine. *It must have a sense of occasion, a sense of drama!*

As professional musician David Lasker said in *Muscle & Fitness*: "A bodybuilding event is a *show!* It takes showmanship to win. You have to think of yourself as a performer . . . when on stage."

You will be nervous everybody is nervous—but the more you have practiced your free posing the better it will appear on the night of the event. And really good music must have audience impact. The music must have forward thrust.

David Lasker elaborated on how to find the right posing music: "Find a piece that starts softly, with only a few instruments playing, then builds to a spine-tingling, goose-bump-raising climax, complete with cymbal crashes and trumpet fanfares. This kind of music has audience impact!"

Each pose has its own character. Match your facial expression to the pose. A front muscular pose mixes well with a broad smile, a swoop into a three-quarter back pose may merge nicely with a concentrated frown. . . .

Strive to give each of your poses its own emotional weight and character while binding them together in the routine. There must be no sign of hesitation; no stumbling, compensation, or adjustment. Never shuffle your feet or realign your costume.

Plunge and sweep; move with the music . . . live and breathe the action. You have only two minutes to tell the tale. Some poses will be long and outstretched, while others will be choppy and brief. Tell it *your* way with vivid imagination, verve, and originality. Tell the audience with your body how enthusiastic you feel about being a bodybuilder. Make it work!

Mohamed Makkawy assists Gladys Portugues perfect a pose.

PUBLICITY

Lori Bowen-Rice

Getting Yourself Known

Publicity is exposure—the art of getting yourself known. Some may call it the pursuit of fame. And fame means that people know what you look like, or at least they know your name.

Most bodybuilders do not understand the importance of publicity, nor do they understand how the process works. Fame has to be strived for, but before you begin trying to get famous you had better make sure you are worth it! The world is full of people who have sought publicity or even had it thrust upon them, but couldn't live up to it when it made them a household name.

Publicity—make no mistake about it—is extremely beneficial for you. Many women eligible for the Ms. Olympia competition or other big contests are not even happy about entering unless they have had good magazine exposure prior to the show. "It keeps us in the public eye," says Candy Csencsits. "And besides, the judges have a preview of what they're going to be seeing at contest time."

In show business, negative publicity is even better than positive publicity for getting exposure. However, bodybuilding has a cleaner image. A woman bodybuilder benefits most when magazine readers see her exercising, running, horseback riding, competing, and enjoying life in general. The IFBB has a strict rule that expels women bodybuilders who bare all on the pages of men's magazines. Women's bodybuilding is a sport and its aim is to be recognized as such worldwide. The IFBB constitution does not embrace the practice of what it considers to be against the interest of the federation and its members.

Premature publicity (seeking to be known before you are ready for it) is worse than no publicity at all. If you just want the satisfaction of seeing your photograph in a bodybuilding magazine, then put on your costume and have your picture taken. Maybe you'll get into print if you send it to a magazine. Don't send it to *Muscle & Fitness* or *MuscleMag International*, expecting it to appear on the next cover of their issue. These magazines have their own in-house photographers, plus a legion of free-lance photographers in *many* countries. Your snapshot could be seen by an editor, who may, if he feels the subject has something, decide to follow through with a request for more information, or even a full-scale photo session with the magazine photographers. However, without the credit of having won state, national, or international bodybuilding contests, you

Georgia Miller-Fudge and Wilt Chamberlain pose for a publicity shot.

would have to be pretty well put together to catch an editor's eye.

Of course, there are many thousands of women who do not want publicity. They train for themselves and their own satisfaction—period! They do not want fame.

Publicity is more for the competing woman, who ultimately wants to achieve the highest goal in bodybuilding, to win the IFBB Ms. Olympia, and then go on to endorse products, give seminars, guest pose, write books and courses, and possibly do film and tele-

must have periodic photo sessions. And when you turn up for these you have to be in the best shape of your life.

Actually, we have known women who have flown thousands of miles to be photographed for a magazine layout only to be turned back at the airport by the photographer. Magazine people can work some pretty good tricks with makeup, lights, and camera techniques, but they cannot work miracles. If you are not in top shape, then your photographs will not show you that way. As phy-

Mary Roberts

vision work. Of course, it could be argued that if all you want is to be a film star, then why go the route of the bodybuilder? Why not just go to acting school? The answer is that probably bodybuilding *is* your first love (as it is with Arnold Schwarzenegger, Gladys Portugues, Candy Csencsits, and Rachel McLish). Your priorities are physical achievement first and foremost.

One of the most important keys to your early publicity is the photo session. If you want regular and ongoing exposure, then you

sique photographer John Balik says: "When a bodybuilder tells me she looks 'ripped to the bone' the photosession is on, but if she tells me that she's looking 'pretty good' . . . I offer to cancel out. I know she's fat."

Being prepared for a successful photo session involves having a fat-free body, an even tan, a good hairstyle, complementary makeup, and appropriate clothing or costumes.

Just winning or doing well in top bodybuilding contests will guarantee you *some*

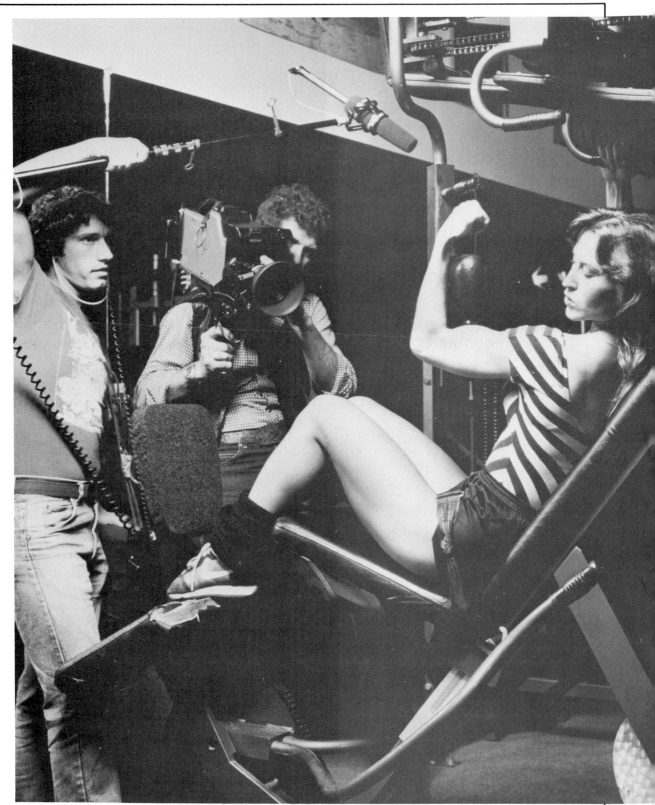

Rachel McLish is very accustomed to posing or working out in front of the camera.

The posedown: Kike Elomaa, Rachel McLish, and Deborah Diana show how it's done.

publicity, but exposure over and above this is often dependent on magazine publishers being made aware of your existence when you are in top shape.

Having your photograph taken can be a time-consuming, monotonous, and ultimately aggravating experience. A session usually lasts hours—or even days—with short breaks. You will be surrounded by cameras, lights, batteries, exercise apparatus, and props. Often it will seem like the same photograph is being taken over and over again. Out of the hundreds of pictures taken at a photo session only a handful may be used—perhaps none. The photographer is doing everything he can

Candy Csencsits

Joe Weider, surrounded by many of the top women bodybuilders, has done more for the sport than any other individual.

Carla Temple

Personal appearances, articles in the world press, radio interviews, and television talk shows don't just happen by accident. They are invariably the result of a publicity agent working on your behalf, arranging a schedule of appearances. Public relations companies are expensive—their fees can be thousands of dollars each month. Appearing on a television talk show to promote your newly released exercise book can increase sales enormously, but the modern business-oriented woman knows that the exposure is wasted if you are not promoting a film, book, a videotape, or some other product that can bring you a direct return.

No one can make it in bodybuilding without good publicity. Those who build great physiques (and even a few who do not) and seek out good publicity for themselves invariably do well.

Ironically, there are a few superb female bodybuilders who do not know how to get good publicity. If they caught on to what Cory Everson, Gladys Portugues, Rachel McLish, and Lori Bowen—just a few of the great women bodybuilders—were doing they would be bodybuilding heroines as well.

Bodybuilding for women is a sensational sport. Naturally, the rewards are dependent on how much effort you are prepared to put into it. If you persevere, you will succeed in building, shaping, and refining your body development to a whole new dynamic appearance. Combine modern bodybuilding methods with sound nutrition and supplementation and you will achieve greatness. Whether you want to compete in women's physique contests, or merely want to keep in shape for your own satisfaction, you will be delighted with your progress.

If you truly want that great-looking body, nothing can stop you. Your enthusiasm will carry you through your workouts, and with that all-encompassing "high" you will reach your goal. Our best wishes are with you in your efforts. Your success is ahead.

to get the best photograph. When you feel like screaming . . . don't. Bear with it. One good picture speaks a thousand words and you will be the one to benefit when it's published.

Beyond the magazines, the cost of publicity gets expensive. Unless you are already a major star in bodybuilding, you will have to pay for your exposure in one way or another.

Winning helps! Mary Roberts hoists her giant trophy.

About the Authors

Ben Weider shakes off any compliments tossed in his direction when it is hinted that he is responsible for starting the current massive surge in the popularity of bodybuilding. "My brother Joe was the initial genius who created the environment for me to work in the field of bodybuilding. He had a burning desire to develop a magnificent physique and began training in a shed in 1934."

Joe started his first magazine in Montreal, Canada, at the age of seventeen, with only seven dollars to his name. It was a simple mimeographed effort, which originally sold for ten cents a copy. It built steadily from there. Today it is known as *Muscle & Fitness* and outsells the world in bodybuilding and physical conditioning publications.

Both Ben and Joe were naturals when it came to business. Although the early years were tough, their ongoing efforts paid off. It was later decided that Joe Weider would open up offices in the United States—first in New York, then in Los Angeles. Ben opted to stay in Canada. While brother Joe was building funds via the lucrative mail-order field, using his profits to improve his bodybuilding magazine, Ben concentrated on developing his own sporting goods business in Montreal. As a result of Ben Weider's excellent managerial skills, the company was almost running itself. This enabled Ben to devote the majority of his time to the promotion of bodybuilding as an accepted world sport. Through his duties as the elected president of the International Federation of Bodybuilders (IFBB), he resolutely set out to legitimize and promote bodybuilding in every part of the globe. His record speaks for itself. He visited over fifty nations to solicit qualified membership, and the IFBB now has chapters in 126 countries. He is at the helm of the sixth-largest sports organization in the world, affiliated to the General Assembly of Sports Federations.

Ben Weider displays the special Joe Weider Mr. Olympia medal.

Ben Weider practices what he preaches. He works out three times a week with weights, does 300 push-ups and 200 sit-ups every day, is happily married to a beautiful French-Canadian, Hugette, and is the father of three children.

He has authored eight books, including *Fit for Life* a program of common-sense techniques and practices for good health. Other books he has authored have been on nutrition and exercise, subjects on which Ben is an acknowledged world authority. His main interest at present is to spread the popularity of bodybuilding by constantly upgrading its acceptance. Although *Olympic Review* magazine (the official publication of the Olympic committee) reports the staging of the IFBB bodybuilding events, bodybuilding is not an Olympic sport. Ben Weider is determined to use all his expertise and influence to change that. "One day," he says knowingly, "the sport of bodybuilding will be an Olympic event." If perseverance has any bearing on the matter, then his dream will come true.

Ben Weider has been honored with the highest civilian award given by the Canadian government, the *Order of Canada*. He has also received the Distinguished Service Award from the United States Sports Academy for his worldwide promotion of bodybuilding.

On the international front he was recently nominated for the Nobel Peace Prize for his ongoing efforts to build better understanding among all people through fitness and bodybuilding. His credo is: "Bodybuilding is good for nation building."

Robert Kennedy is the publisher of his own bodybuilding magazine, *MuscleMag International*. It was founded in 1974 on a shoestring budget (he had 100,000 printed, distributed them via newsstands, and crossed his fingers), and it continues to grow steadily in sales throughout the world. "*MuscleMag International* is a considerably smaller voice than Weider's *Muscle & Fitness*," says Kennedy, "but we do our best to supply the needs of hardcore male and female bodybuilders."

Robert Kennedy is British by origin, his mother being English and his father Austrian. As an only child, he grew up in England as a pupil in his mother's preparatory school in Thetford, Norfolk, and eventually passed through Culford Public School to Norwich College of Art where he obtained the highest British government art award: the National Diploma in Design. In addition he attended universities in Salzburg, Austria; Lausanne, Switzerland; and Loughborough Physical Training College in England.

Robert Kennedy's interests are diverse and his talents are considerable. He is an accomplished artist and sculptor, having exhibited and won awards for his works for more than twenty-five years. He has had several one-man painting exhibitions in London, Austria, and Canada.

His avid interest in bodybuilding, a sport which he still practices to this day, has made him one of the most knowledgeable people in the field. He has written many books, the most successful of which are: *Start Bodybuilding*, *Hardcore Bodybuilding*, *Beef It!*, and *Unleashing the Wild Physique*, the latter of which he co-authored with veteran physical-culture expert Vince Gironda. All books were published by the Sterling Publishing Co., Inc., in New York City.

Like Ben Weider, Robert Kennedy is a friend to many of the world's top competing bodybuilders and he is an acknowledged supporter of the IFBB and Ben's endless efforts to bring bodybuilding to the world.

Ironically, both Weider and Kennedy could be seen by outsiders as adversaries since they are business competitors in the bodybuilding field.

"The truth is," says Kennedy, "that Ben and I have a camaraderie that supersedes practical business activity. We both love the sport of bodybuilding and have mutually decided to pool our knowledge to make *Pumping Up! Super Shaping the Feminine Physique* the bible of women's bodybuilding."

Robert Kennedy looks at Beef It!—*one of his many best-selling books.*

Index